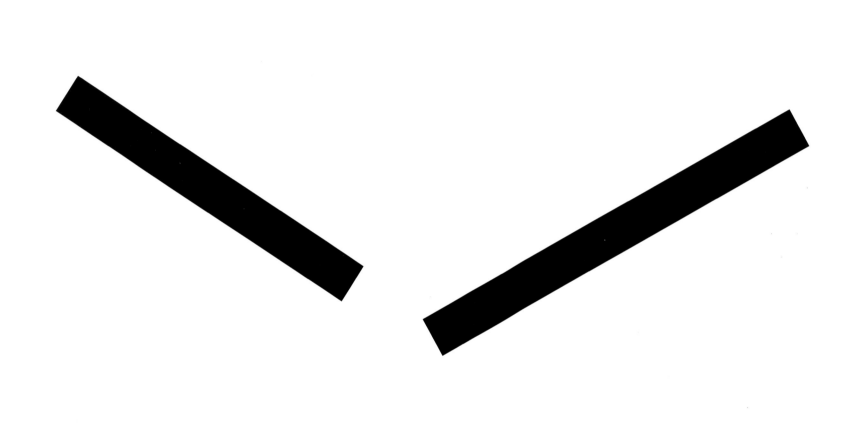

BREAKING GROUND

ARCHITECTURE BY WOMEN

Φ

JANE HALL

WOULD THEY STILL CALL ME A DIVA?

On hearing that São Paulo City Hall intended to build restrooms below the belvedere on Avenida Paulista in downtown São Paulo, Italo-Brazilian architect Lina Bo Bardi visited the city's mayor, Ademar Pereira de Barros, laying in front of him plans for a new building. The sketches depicted a new design for the São Paulo Museum of Art (1968), an institution that Bo Bardi had helped to found over a decade earlier.[1] The proposal would maintain the view across São Paulo by implementing the largest concrete span in the world, elevating the structure to provide a generous public space below. Bo Bardi enlisted an influential journalist, who offered media support in return for the withdrawal of the city's original plans,[2] which, according to Bo Bardi, the mayor had agreed to 'without even looking at the drawing'.[3] Despite her proposing a design for what would become one of the most influential and recognizable buildings in Latin America (pp. 28–9), winning the job through her own astute negotiation, Bo Bardi's husband, Pietro Maria Bardi, rejected his wife's initial plan as 'the beautiful dream of a woman'.[4] Her husband's comment can be read into in a number of ways; language was deployed differently then (1959) and, unsurprisingly for a man born at the turn of the twentieth century, Pietro's sexism is well documented. Yet there is much to suggest that the couple in fact had a radical marriage, as creative peers in a union that spanned half a century, with Bo Bardi the beneficiary of the social position and connections to build under her own name. Today, however, Bo Bardi's narrative is one of design genius trumping male authority, with her achievements attributed to her forceful nature in spite of, rather than because of, her gender.

Bo Bardi's legacy reflects the gendered difference in the way in which women architects are portrayed. Often painted as a feminized version of a hyper-masculine character, women architects are actively judged on their personality before they are on their buildings.[5] Desiring no difference between the sexes, however, runs the risk of recognizing the professional title of architect as male, rather than acknowledging that it could mean something – *anything* – else. Indeed, asking women to account for the significance of their own gender is a way of not hearing about them as architects at all. Yet many women in practice remain defiant, asserting that their sex and gender are an important facet of their work. Increasingly, this is because history tells us that there have always been many women, such as Bo Bardi, who established themselves in practice. In the twentieth century, we had Jane Drew (p. 56), Ray Eames (p. 57), Eileen Gray (p. 82)

and Alison Smithson (p. 181) – all of whose names are well known – while in the twenty-first, we have had (among others) Zaha (p. 83), the ubiquity of her success relieving her of the need for a last name. However, the experiences of the majority of women in, and *remaining in*, architecture do not reflect such straightforward histories. Despite the impressive nature of the work produced by the women we *do* know about, we shouldn't simply trust the visibility of a few as an obvious signifier of progress. This is important because the process of talking about being a woman in architecture is not just about gaining parity in terms of numbers but is also a strategy for thinking more broadly about what it means to be an architect living and working today.

At the heart of this problem is the retelling of architectural history, and its preoccupation with singularity in the attribution of authorship of a building. In saying this, given the increasing complexity of contemporary identity categories is there value in re-attributing authorship today? Or indeed drawing attention to an individual at all, particularly based solely on their sex? The simple answer is that because authorship, over and over again, has been attributed, celebrated and promoted by and on behalf of men, this history needs correction.[6] Charles Eames's quip that 'anything I can do Ray can do better' is an acknowledgement of his wife's abilities, yet solely in relation to his own – while Eileen Gray's house E-1027 was made famous in part because of Swiss master Le Corbusier's vandalism of it.[7] French architect Charlotte Perriand (p. 148), another woman whose career cannot so easily be separated from Le Corbusier's, is eclipsed in the same way that Anne Tyng's twenty-eight years spent working with Louis Kahn, and the proliferation of her own designs, are almost completely unknown. So, while the successes of many female architects are increasingly being acknowledged, the stories that we hear are primarily about those who have in some way been associated with the (male) 'giants' of twentieth-century modern architecture, meaning that they are situated comfortably within the accepted framework of Western cultural discourse. Conversely, many accomplished and successful women have been written out of history precisely because of their proximity to more famous men, rather than their place being in any way assured by it. While the Dutch artist Madelon Vriesendorp is known for her early collaboration and partnership with Office for Metropolitan Architecture (OMA) co-founder Rem Koolhaas, her influential, poetic and satirically precise drawing titled *Fragrant Délit*, depicting two New York skyscrapers post-copulation, has become a defining image of *his* work, rather than of hers.[8] Vriesendorp's contribution to the young OMA has to be constantly reasserted.

Recently, editing women architects out of history has been a more deliberate act. In what can arguably be described as a violent misuse of Photoshop (compounded by the fact that it was so well done), Patty Hopkins (p. 95), who won the RIBA Royal Gold Medal for architecture in 1994, was removed from a press shot showing her with a number of famed male colleagues including her own husband, Michael Hopkins, with whom she had built an entire career and, indeed, shared the award.[9] Such erasure perhaps remains most felt in the awards system, where dedicated prizes for women highlight their work but legitimize their absence from the more prestigious accolades. In 2012, the oversight in failing to award Lu Wenyu (p. 123) of Amateur Architecture Studio the Pritzker Prize in recognition of her work alongside partner Wang Shu only echoes the invisibility of Denise Scott Brown (p. 168) from her partner Robert Venturi's 1999 success.[10] These are suspicious omissions. Both are women who have supposedly 'made it' in a man's world, yet their right to occupy such space remains constantly subject to revision. The striking image of Sri Lankan architect Minnette de Silva (p. 177) pictured dressed in a sari, sitting at the front of the first post-war meeting of the International Congresses of Modern Architecture, or Congrès Internationaux d'Architecture Moderne, at Bridgwater, UK, in 1947, with Le Corbusier conspicuous in the background, is little known, serving as a reminder that received history is a selective record wherein to be female in architecture is to occupy the margins.[11]

This book, then, does not support the idea of 'women' as an aesthetic category but rather presents an architectural history of buildings through a female lens. In doing so, this volume highlights the work of extraordinary women under-represented in their lifetimes, and now largely lost to traditional forms of history-making. The book, however, does not rewrite these histories but seeks to subvert existing historiographies in order to show that women were no more sole authors of buildings than were their male counterparts, but that they were there alongside the men, working in parallel and in collaboration. A great example of this is Lilly Reich's part in designing the 'Barcelona' chair, so named after the Barcelona Pavilion (1929), for which her partner, Ludwig Mies van der Rohe, tends to get full credit (p. 160). Another is MJ Long's contribution to the design of the British Library (1998), a project under-

taken over a thirty-year period by the office of Colin St John Wilson but largely executed by Long (p. 121) – as is the significance of Jane Drew's role in what is widely considered to be Le Corbusier's defining built urban project, the masterplanning and construction of Chandigarh (1953) in India. Often overlooked, Drew was in fact responsible for recommending Le Corbusier for the job. Along with her partner, Maxwell Fry, Drew would spend three years continually working on the city, with Le Corbusier visiting only during the cooler months – leading Fry to state later, 'I had to fight him [Le Corbusier] because he is a little bit of a megalomaniac. I said, a city should be made by several people, not one. And, in any case, we're here.'[12]

A bias towards male narratives during the twentieth century has meant that women like Drew were less visible than their male counterparts, regardless of their own sense of equity in their daily working lives. In many ways, the synchronicity of architecture husband-and-wife teams makes it a futile task to separate individual contributions from the collective identity for which their work is known. The inclusion of a number of female 'halves' in this book does not seek to distort these unions but exists to emphasize that in many ways it is impossible to disentangle the interconnected working relationship of women from those with whom they work. What is important, then, is a greater recognition of the dynamics of such partnerships. A good example is provided by English architects Alison and Peter Smithson. On occasion, each pointed to the authorial merits of the other – yet largely they presented themselves intentionally as a singular entity, their direct influence on one another positioned as central to how we should understand their architecture. Radically for a young couple in the 1950s and early 60s, both Smithsons shouldered equal responsibility for the care of their three children, simultaneously blending their home with their office life; they even occasionally involved their children in a project's design. Indeed, their family arrangements had a direct impact on their ability to produce architecture. They worked on only one project at a time, completing a large-scale building once every ten years. Alison stated herself that the couple were frugal in the way the pair balanced their family with work, intentionally avoiding private schooling – her initial preference for their children's education – so as to give the pair greater freedom to design.[13]

Such blurring of work and home life is less possible in non-marital unions. Practices today, often made up of a number of partners whose identities are denoted by the contribution of their last name to an acronym, cannot so readily rely on bending the office to the will of their personal proclivities. For some reason, attribution of authorship also becomes more slippery in these types of company structures. A woman's contributions are more carefully scrutinized when her name is not individualized: which bit did she do? Which building is hers? This posed a real problem in researching this book, with many practices themselves rejecting the inclusion of certain works due to their female partner's lack of involvement in a building's design, overlooking the fact that her role enables design activity simply to take place. Owing to a tendency out of step with the actuality of contemporary practice and symptomatic of an outdated desire to highlight singularity and name it, women are subject to the ongoing propensity to treat the act of design as the essential contribution to the built object rather than the 'back end' of managing architectural production. In a climate in which the industry demands attributes that balance creative expression with business acumen, the inclusion in this book of women who run practices – either alone or collaboratively, with a number of colleagues of different genders – is intended to promote an expanded idea of how architecture in reality gets made.

However, the focus on built works in this book perhaps disguises the fact that historically, for many women working in and around the profession, architecture-as-building is not a central occupation. The flexibility of non-studio-based working environments and barriers to access in the building industry have meant that women, out of necessity, have been heavily influential in shaping theoretical discourse rather than construction. Jane Jacobs, one of the most influential American writers of the twentieth century, who promoted the street life around her Greenwich Village home in Manhattan, advocated a form of architecture preoccupied with everyday and participatory approaches to design – her writing on urbanism is widely read and globally disseminated to this day. In an age when New York public official Robert Moses was single-handedly reshaping the city with bold infrastructural gestures, Jacobs's view was a refreshing antidote based on observations of the way in which people actually lived. In order to capture the importance of those such as Jacobs, this book includes a reading list and notes that describe the work of others who have contributed to architectural discourse in what can be thought of as maybe quieter, but equally influential, ways. For example, the UK-based feminist design cooperative

MATRIX, a product of the women's liberation movement in the 1980s, worked together to empower women to take control over their built environment by exploring the belief that the social construction of gender had led to fundamentally different design needs for women.[14] The cooperative's legacy is most effectively seen in its teaching and publishing of that period, and can now be found in the ongoing work of subsequent groups like Taking Place.[15]

Groups such as these have traditionally relied heavily on the university as a site of radical thinking, as a means to bridge the gap between theory and practice. Until recently not so beholden to market forces as architectural practice, academic environments have proven spaces where being and thinking differently are positive, even complementary, attributes. For example, architectural historian Jane Rendell has for a long time been a driving force at University College London, publishing important texts on what she refers to as a 'feminist critical spatial practice', while in the US Beatriz Colomina, professor of architecture at Princeton University, is the author of *Sexuality & Space* (1992), a definitive book on how gender is spatially inscribed.[16] Peggy Deamer and Keller Easterling at Yale University have fundamentally changed how we think about labour in practice and the infrastructural scale of architecture respectively, while Amale Andraos (p. 13) and Mónica Ponce de León (p. 154) hold tenure as heads of department at influential Ivy League schools. Indeed, Elizabeth Diller (p. 54), partner at Diller Scofidio + Renfro, credits her own time at Cooper Union for her practice's conceptual approach to architecture, influenced also by her early career as an artist. As a space of extreme privilege, however, higher education can only do so much to begin a process of change because of its limited access for a number of marginal groups – not least for women, and particularly women of colour. A number of platforms have been launched in order to address this dilemma within educational settings, designed specifically to widen the spatial reach of feminism in architecture. Two Swedish groups – FATALE, based at KTH Royal Institute of Technology in Stockholm, and MYCKET, initiated in 2012 by a small group of designers, architects and artists – connect anti-racism and LGBTQIA perspectives with both architectural theory and practice. In Australia, Parlour operates a more normative online platform with its slogan 'Women, Equity, Architecture' representing its ambition to make women more visible in the workplace.[17] All free and easily accessible online, these sites tell us not only that such discourse has a mainstream appeal but also that, due to their increasing curation by a much younger and significantly less white generation than hitherto, they also encompass non-binary and allied perspectives.

The striking invisibility in a mainstream context of women working across the African continent, and in Central and Southeast Asia particularly, made this book difficult to research. This imbalance in representation only reinforces the notion that the acceptance of women in architectural practice is conditional on location and shaped by a colonial legacy. More work needs to be done to investigate the politics of this multi-locality, and how groups such as the newly founded Black Females in Architecture in London and Khensani de Klerk's Matri-(Archi)tecture in Cape Town can better provide solidarity and support for those whose identities might not reflect that of the majority.[18] Returning to Minnette de Silva, when she self-defines as an 'Asian Woman Architect' she focuses attention on the intersection of her gender and geographic origins.[19] Her approach is one that we must admire; at a time when the world is being torn apart by identity politics, the simple act of acknowledging women as authors of buildings, and the spaces in which they do this, is itself a necessary political act. What is at stake, then, is the issue of how easy it is for women to become lost in the various structures that govern how architecture is produced and then communicated. Intentionally or not, the writing of this history has been a process of exclusion rather than inclusion. This book argues that we must find other forms of representation and other types of language with which to talk about becoming a woman in design, advancing the call for alternative approaches to architecture that seek out difference without negating the significance of the work of women involved in practices that do conform to the status quo.

Breaking Ground is also a celebration of some of us that have come before. Jadwiga Grabowska-Hawrylak (p. 81), Raili Pietilä (p. 149), Flora Ruchat-Roncati (p. 164) and, more recently, Beate Hølmebakk (p. 94), Anupama Kundoo (p. 111), Marina Tabassum (p. 184) and Yui Tezuka (p. 188) are among my personal favourites included in the following pages. Much of their work I would have been unlikely to have seen at all if it hadn't been for the opportunity to dedicate time to this topic. The works of these architects, organized alphabetically, are shown alongside a short but comprehensive biography of each in order to better contextualize each woman's role and, where appropriate, her connection to the projects presented. Collaborating on this book with a number of others – both male and female – in my own practice, Assemble, we have collectively come to conclude that the comparably significant number of women working in architecture today, coupled with the change and growth in types of firms, has allowed women not only to progress but also to become less visible. Perhaps this is a sign of equality. Or maybe this is an illusion that supports the assertion made by many women in architecture that there is little need to define one's own identity as female, let alone any other sex and gender. In a world where the many differences between women highlight the fact that this can only be true for a privileged few, a more complex narrative, which reveals the intersectional lived experiences of those in the profession, is urgently needed. A gender-neutral industry – indeed, a gender-neutral built environment – if desired, cannot be simply willed into existence. It must be fought for. Invisibility is a sign that there is still much more work to do.

— Dr Jane Hall and Audrey Thomas-Hayes

I AM NOT A FEMALE ARCHITECT. I AM AN ARCHITECT.

Dorte Mandrup

AMALE ANDRAOS

WORKac

Born in Lebanon, architect, writer and educator
Andraos (b. 1973) lived and practised in Saudi Arabia,
France, Canada and the Netherlands before co-
founding WORKac in New York in 2003 with Dan Wood.
The international firm has won acclaim for projects
that examine the connection between urban and
natural environments. In 2014, Andraos became dean
of the Columbia Graduate School of Architecture in
New York, the first woman to hold the post, where
she is credited with furthering the school's global and
environmental engagement.

Museum Garage, Miami, Florida, USA, 2018

BRIT ANDRESEN

Andresen O'Gorman Architects

Norway-born Australian architect Andresen
(b. 1945) set up Andresen O'Gorman Architects with
Peter O'Gorman in Australia in 1980, specializing
in residential projects. Their practice is described
as being unique for its sensitivity to place, scholarly
preoccupations and unusual intelligence; for the
Ocean View Farmhouse (below), the architects chose
materials with colours derived from the landscape –
a recurring feature in their work. Andresen was the
first woman recipient of the Australian Institute of
Architects' Gold Medal in 2002.

Ocean View Farmhouse, Mount Mee, Queensland,
Australia, 1995

SANDRA BARCLAY

Barclay & Crousse

Barclay (b. 1967) studied architecture in Lima, Peru, and Paris, France, before founding the architecture practice Barclay & Crousse with Jean Pierre Crousse in 1994. Orignally based in Paris, the office moved to Lima in 2006. The studio's work explores the bonds between landscape, climate and architecture. Barclay contributed to the Peruvian entry for the Venice Architecture Biennale in 2012 and curated Peru's pavilion in 2016. In 2018 she won the Architect of the Year prize from the Women in Architecture awards.

↓   Paracas Museum, Paracas, Peru, 2016
↓↓ University Facilities UDEP, Piura, Peru, 2016

JULIA BARFIELD

Marks Barfield Architects

Barfield (b. 1952) is best known as the co-creator of the London Eye (opposite), a cantilevered observation wheel, which she designed with David Marks. Barfield graduated from the Architectural Association School of Architecture in London in 1978 and later worked for Norman Foster for nine years. Barfield and Marks established Marks Barfield Architects in 1989 with projects across all sectors, and they were both awarded MBEs (Members of the Order of the British Empire) in 2000. They also designed the i360 viewing tower in Brighton, UK (2016).

← London Eye, London, England, UK, 2000

ELIANA BELTRÁN, CATALINA PATIÑO AND VIVIANA PEÑA

Ctrl G

Colombian architects Beltrán (b. 1984), Patiño (b. 1983) and Peña (b. 1984) graduated from the Pontifical Bolivarian University in Medellín, Colombia, in 2006. They founded Ctrl G in 2008 when they were chosen to design two kindergartens – in Pajarito La Aurora (below) and San Antonio de Prado (2011) – which are inspired by the concept of 'union and repetition'. They have since been involved in many public projects, including innovative educational parks and museums.

↓ Jardín Infantil Pajarito La Aurora, Medellín, Colombia, 2011, with Federico Mesa, Plan:b

DEBORAH BERKE

Deborah Berke Partners

Berke (b. 1954) graduated from the Rhode Island School of Design in the US in both fine art (1975) and architecture (1977). She founded her own practice in New York, Deborah Berke Partners, whose work includes the Irwin Union Bank (below), made of a glass volume on top of a brick volume, and various 21c Museum Hotels across the US (2006–). In 2016 she was appointed dean at the Yale School of Architecture, and in 2012 she was the inaugural recipient of the Berkeley-Rupp Prize, which promotes sustainability, the community and women in architecture.

↓   Irwin Union Bank, Columbus, Indiana, USA, 2006

TATIANA BILBAO

Tatiana Bilbao Estudio

The work of Mexican-born and based Bilbao (b. 1972) is informed by deep field research and collaborations with artists, including Gabriel Orozco and Ai Weiwei, as well as philosophers, sociologists and gardeners. Bilbao was the recipient of the Berliner Kunstpreis in 2012 and, in 2014, the Global Award for Sustainable Architecture. She currently heads the firm Tatiana Bilbao Estudio, founded in 2004, which she runs with partners David Vaner and her sister Catia Bilbao.

→   Los Terrenos, San Pedro Garza García, Mexico, 2016
↘   Bioinnova, Monterrey Institute of Technology, Culiacán, Mexico, 2012

MARGARET JUSTIN
BLANCO WHITE

Blanco White (1911–2001) was a Scottish architect who graduated from the Architectural Association School of Architecture in London in 1934. She was best known for the Modernist houses she designed in Cambridge – particularly the timber-faced Shawms residence (below), which has since been granted heritage listing. She subsequently collaborated with architects Mary Medd (p. 131) and Ernö Goldfinger on pioneering designs for housing, educational and community buildings. She was awarded an OBE (Officer of the Order of the British Empire) in 1973.

Shawms, Conduit Head Road, Cambridge, England, UK, 1938

CAMILLA BLOCK

Durbach Block Jaggers

South African-born Block (n.d.) moved to Australia when she was twelve. With Neil Durbach and David Jaggers, she is one of three directors of Durbach Block Jaggers, a practice co-founded in Sydney in 1998. Block has been a design principal in all of the practice's major projects, including the Thomas Street Science Building at the University of Technology Sydney (2015) and the Olympics Amenities Buildings (2000), both in Sydney. Their work often integrates landscape and architecture, as seen in the Holman House (below), which perches over the Tasman Sea.

Holman House, Sydney, NSW, Australia, 2016

NATALIE DE BLOIS

Skidmore, Owings & Merrill (SOM)

De Blois (1921–2013) graduated from Columbia University in New York in 1944, and was a leading light in America's mid-twentieth-century male-dominated architecture scene. In particular, she was an important designer of corporate Modernist buildings, including the Union Carbide Corporation Headquarters (opposite) and the Pepsi-Cola Headquarters (1960, with Gordon Bunshaft) – both in New York, and both of which she designed while working for SOM. She moved to the firm's Chicago office in 1974 and founded the Chicago Women in Architecture organization.

← Union Carbide Corporation Headquarters, New York City, New York, USA, 1960

SHIRLEY BLUMBERG

KPMB Architects

Blumberg (b. 1952) studied architecture at the University of Cape Town in South Africa and, after emigrating to Canada, completed her education at the University of Toronto. In 1987, she co-founded the Toronto-based practice of KPMB. Recognized for her virtuosic use of materials, she is the recipient of numerous awards including a Governor General's Medal, an American Institute of Architects Honor Award and a Royal Institute of British Architects International Award.

↓ Remai Modern, Saskatoon, Saskatchewan, Canada, 2017, with Architecture49

LINA BO BARDI

Bo Bardi (1914–92), an Italian-born Brazilian designer, was one of the most important architects of the twentieth century. Her house, Casa de Vidro (below), is considered a Modernist masterpiece, while the São Paulo Museum of Art (overleaf) and SESC Pompéia leisure centre (opposite) – both in Brazil's most populous city – are lauded as two of the best examples of Brutalist architecture in the canon. In all of her work – which also included furniture, theatre and jewellery design – she promoted the social and cultural benefits of architecture and design.

↓   Casa de Vidro, São Paulo, Brazil, 1951
→   SESC Pompéia, São Paulo, Brazil, 1986
↓↓ São Paulo Museum of Art, São Paulo, Brazil, 1968

CINI BOERI

Cini Boeri Architetti

A leading figure in Italian design, Boeri (b. 1924) graduated from the Politecnico di Milano in 1951. After a brief period working for Gio Ponti, she collaborated with Marco Zanuso. Her own practice, established in 1963, produces work across the fields of architecture, furniture design and industrial design for clients such as Knoll and Arflex. Boeri has lectured around the world – particularly in the US and Brazil. Her most prestigious awards include the Compasso d'Oro in 1979 and, in 2008, a Lifetime Achievement Award from the Italian Cultural Institute of Los Angeles.

Casa Rotonda, La Maddalena, Italy, 1967

ELISABETH BÖHM

Böhm Studio

Elisabeth Böhm (1921–2012) was a German architect who collaborated on many projects with Gottfried Böhm – the Bensberg Town Hall (below) is considered a masterpiece of humanist Brutalism. Böhm largely concentrated on housing projects and gained renown for the sensitive contemporary additions that she made to cultural landmarks and for imposing her own style on interiors, such as the extension to Godesburg Castle near Bonn (1959).

Bensberg Town Hall, Bergisch Gladbach, Germany, 1967

THE GENDER IMBALANCE IN THE FIELD OF ARCHITECTURE IS EXAGGERATED BY A LACK OF ROLE MODELS. I HAD NO FEMALE ROLE MODELS.

Toshiko Mori

TERESA BORSUK

Pollard Thomas Edwards

Borsuk (b. 1956) joined London-based firm Pollard Thomas Edwards in 1984 after studying at the Bartlett School of Architecture (University College London). Her commitment to improving gender equality has seen the proportion of female staff rise to over fifty per cent within the firm. Borsuk's experience spans the housing, regeneration and mixed-use sectors, including award-winning projects The Granary (below) and The Avenue (2014). She received the Architect of the Year prize from the Women in Architecture awards in 2015.

The Granary, London, England, UK, 2011

LOUISE BRAVERMAN

Louise Braverman Architect

Braverman (b. 1948) graduated from the Yale School
of Architecture and established her own practice
in New York in 1991. Among her notable projects are
Poets House in Manhattan's financial district (2009),
a sustainable housing complex for health workers
in a village in Burundi (2013) and the Centro de Artes
Nadir Afonso (below). Braverman's company has
exhibited at numerous Venice architecture biennales,
and has won awards from the Boston Society
of Architects and the Chicago Athenaeum. She is
a Fellow of the American Institute of Architects.

Centro de Artes Nadir Afonso, Boticas, Portugal, 2013

ALISON BROOKS

Alison Brooks Architects

Brooks (b. 1962) is an internationally renowned UK-based architect, best known for her work in housing, regeneration and education. Her studio has created a variety of works, from The Smile (below), a banana-like pavilion for the 2016 London Design Festival, to a campus for Exeter College at the University of Oxford (2017). She is the only British architect to have won all three of the UK's most prestigious architecture awards: the Stirling Prize, the Manser Medal and the Stephen Lawrence Prize. In 2013 she received the Architect of the Year prize from the Women in Architecture awards.

The Smile, London, England, UK, 2016

BARBARA BRUKALSKA

Polish architect and interior designer Brukalska (1899–1980) was a member of the avant-garde Praesens group before World War II along with renowned architects Stanisław Brukalski, Helena and Szymon Syrkus, and Józef Szanajca, among others. The group, heavily influenced by Le Corbusier, championed functional housing for the masses that could be built cheaply. Brukalska advocated practical furnishings and equipment, and spent several years designing the interiors of passenger ships. She was the first woman to be appointed professor at the Warsaw University of Technology.

Willa Brukalskich, Warsaw, Poland, 1929

GLORIA CABRAL

Gabinete de Arquitectura

Cabral (b. 1982) was born in São Paulo, Brazil, but moved to Paraguay at the age of six. She joined Gabinete de Arquitectura in Asunción as an intern in 2003, and now jointly runs the practice. She is a protégé of Swiss architect Peter Zumthor and is known for working with modest materials, such as Paraguayan brick, in inventive ways. The practice won a Golden Lion at the 2016 Venice Architecture Biennale, and Cabral won the Moira Gemmill Prize for Emerging Architecture from the Women in Architecture awards in 2018.

Quincho Tía Coral, Asunción, Paraguay, 2015

FERNANDA CANALES

Fernanda Canales Arquitectura

Canales (b. 1974) was born in Mexico City and studied at the city's Ibero-American University, graduating in 1997. She took up the role of professor at the university, and worked in Tokyo for Toyo Ito and in Barcelona for Ignasi de Solà-Morales. She set up her own practice in Mexico City in 1996, and has since been recognized for seeing each project as an opportunity to narrow the gap between what we build and where we actually want to live. Canales has published several books about Mexican architecture, linking the field to urban planning and design.

Bruma House, Estado de México, Mexico, 2017, with Claudia Rodríguez

LUCÍA CANO

SelgasCano

Cano (b. 1965) was born in Madrid and established SelgasCano – a Spain-based studio – with José Selgas in 1998. The firm's projects include the Plasencia Auditorium and Congress Centre (2017), shortlisted for the European Union Mies van der Rohe Award 2019. SelgasCano is renowned for its use of bright colours and innovative materials, evident in their amorphous, multicoloured designs of the Mérida Factory Youth Movement (below). The firm was the first Spanish practice asked to design the Serpentine Pavilion in London (2015).

Mérida Factory Youth Movement, Mérida, Spain, 2011

GABRIELA CARRILLO

Taller de Arquitectura Mauricio Rocha +
Gabriela Carrillo

Mexican architect Carrillo (b. 1978) graduated from
the National Autonomous University of Mexico and
began collaborating with Mauricio Rocha in 2001. They
formally established their firm in Mexico City in 2011,
building a reputation for sensitivity to contemporary
architecture's place within its setting. They won the
prestigious Emerging Voices in Architecture award in
2014. For her work on the Pátzcuaro Criminal Courts
(below), Carrillo was named Architect of the Year in the
2017 Women in Architecture awards.

Pátzcuaro Criminal Courts, Pátzcuaro, Mexico, 2015

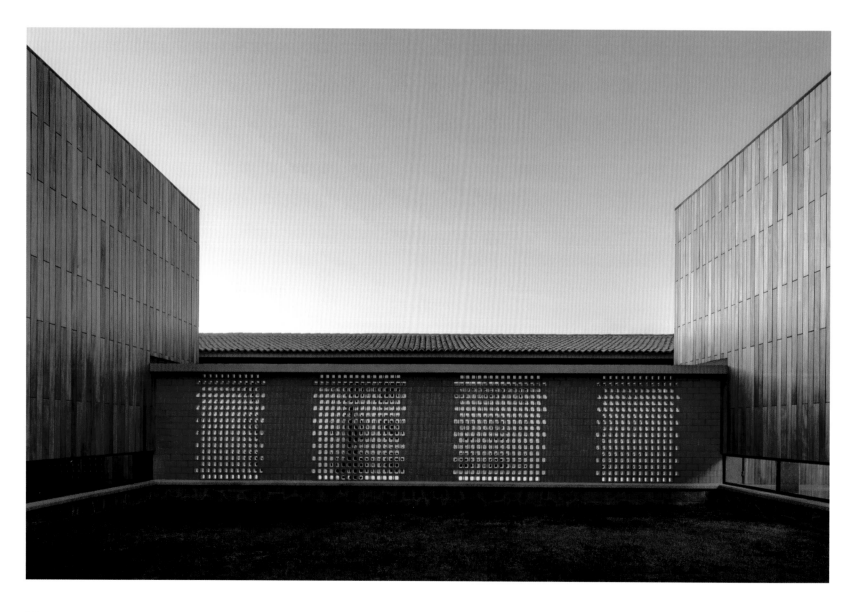

ALICE CASEY

TAKA Architects

Casey (b. 1978) graduated from the Dublin Institute of Technology in 2003 and subsequently co-founded Dublin-based TAKA Architects with Cian Deegan in 2006. Recognized for producing work that is marked by a unique materiality, the practice became the youngest ever representatives of Ireland at the Venice Architecture Biennale in 2008 as part of *The Lives of Spaces* exhibition. They have completed a number of award-winning projects, including the Merrion Cricket Club (below), which distorts the form of an archetypal pavilion, House 1 and House 2 (2009) as well as House 4 (2011) – all in the Irish capital.

Merrion Cricket Club, Dublin, Ireland, 2014

SOOK HEE CHUN

WISE Architecture

Sook Hee Chun (n.d.) studied at Ewha Women's
University, South Korea, and Princeton University
in the US before establishing WISE Architecture with
Young Jang in 2008. Though initially focusing on
smaller, residential projects that drew on the 'everyday
architecture' of Seoul, the practice has expanded to
include works that range from large-scale commercial
and cultural buildings to exhibitions and installations.
WISE was awarded the Seoul City Architectural Award
for the Museum of War and Women's Human Rights
(2012) in Seoul in 2012.

←   ABC Building, Seoul, South Korea, 2012

ALTUĞ ÇINICI

Çinici Architects

Altuğ Çinici (b. 1935) co-founded an architectural
practice with Behruz Çinici, shortly after graduating
from the Istanbul Technical University in 1959. Their
practice specialized in educational and government
projects, challenging the International Style that
was popular at the time. Since then, the firm has won
many prestigious honours for its impact on Turkish
architecture – including the Simavi Foundation Award
(1985), Iş Bank Award (1986), the National Architecture
Award (1994) and the Aga Khan Award (1995).

↓   METU Faculty of Architecture Building, Ankara,
Turkey, 1963

LISE ANNE COUTURE

Asymptote Architecture

Couture (b. 1959) was born in Montreal and co-founded
Asymptote Architecture in New York with Hani Rashid.
The practice's projects range from architecture to art
installations, masterplans and industrial design, and
the studio's early unbuilt, often provocative experiments
in the digital realm are still influential. Couture has
taught at Yale and Harvard, among other academic
institutions, and is a professor at Columbia University.
Couture and Rashid were named by *Time* magazine
as leaders in innovation for the twenty-first century,
and are joint recipients of the prestigious Frederick
Kiesler Prize for contributions to art and architecture.

HydraPier, Haarlemmermeer, The Netherlands, 2002

SUMAYA DABBAGH

Dabbagh Architects

Dabbagh (n.d.) is a Saudi-born architect who
founded her eponymous practice in Dubai in 2008
after training as an architect in Bath, UK, and
Paris, France. As chair of the Royal Institute of British
Architects Gulf chapter, Dabbagh plays an active role
in encouraging diversity within, and celebrating the
local culture of, that region. Her design for the Mleiha
Archaeological Centre (below), curvilinear in plan
and built largely from sandstone, was shortlisted for
an award at the 2017 World Architecture Festival.

Mleiha Archaeological Centre, Sharjah, United Arab
Emirates, 2016

DANG QUN

MAD Architects

Born in Shanghai, Dang Qun (n.d.) is a principal
partner at MAD Architects – known for its futuristic,
organic designs – where she oversees corporate
operations and project management. MAD's philosophy
is to 'create a balance between humanity, the city,
and the environment', and Dang Qun endeavours
to pioneer technical innovation and 'green' architecture
in each project. She graduated from Iowa State
University in 2000; she has taught there, as well as
at the Pratt Institute in New York.

↓   Ordos Museum, Ordos, Inner Mongolia, China, 2011
→   Absolute Towers, Mississauga, Ontario, Canada, 2012

SHARON DAVIS

Sharon Davis Design

Davis (b. 1960) founded her New York-based studio, Sharon Davis Design, in 2007. Following a successful career in finance, she redirected her professional focus to the built environment and Davis subsequently graduated with a degree from Columbia University in 2006. Davis received the Lucille Smyser Lowenfish Memorial Prize from Columbia University in 2006 and the Women for Women Active Citizens Award. Her firm works with non-profit, public and private clients, helping to improve lives in Nepal, Rwanda and beyond.

↓   Rwandan Share Houses, Rwinkwavu, Rwanda, 2015

ODILE DECQ

Studio Odile Decq

Radical French architect Decq (b. 1955) studied architecture in Rennes, in north-west France, and then Paris, before setting up ODBC with Benoît Cornette in 1978. The duo made an impact on the architecture scene in France in the early 1990s, before Cornette was tragically killed in a car accident in 1998. Decq was awarded the Jane Drew Prize in 2016 for promoting the role of women in architecture. She has taught several generations of students at universities around the world, and in 2014 Decq launched the Confluence Institute, a private architecture school in Lyon, France.

→   Saint-Ange Residence, Seyssins, France, 2015
↘   Frac Bretagne, Rennes, France, 2012

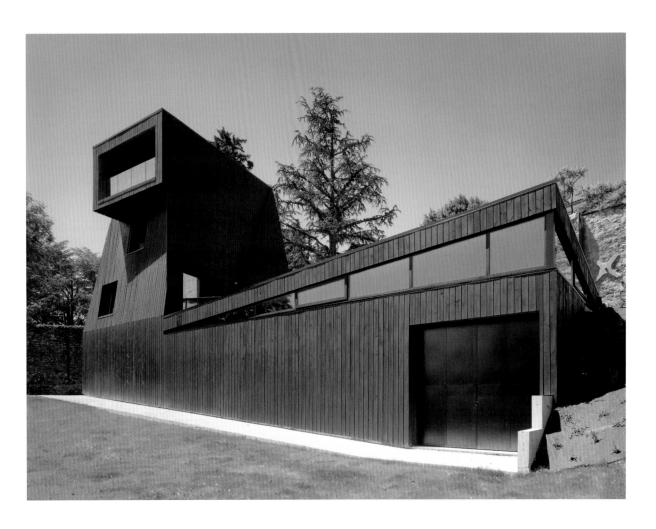

AS A WOMAN IN ARCHITECTURE, YOU'RE ALWAYS AN OUTSIDER. IT'S OKAY, I LIKE BEING ON THE EDGE.

Zaha Hadid

ANGELA DEUBER

Angela Deuber Architect

Deuber (b. 1975) graduated from the ETH (Federal Institute of Technology) Zurich and founded Angela Deuber Architect in 2006, based in Chur, Switzerland. Her practice emphasizes construction and structural research. Deuber was awarded the arcVision Prize – Women and Architecture in 2015 and invited to exhibit at the 2018 Venice Architecture Biennale, in which she presented large-scale drawings for her school in Thal (below). She is visiting professor at the Accademia di Architettura in Mendrisio, Switzerland, and at the Oslo School of Architecture and Design, Norway.

School in Thal, St Gallen, Switzerland, 2014

ELIZABETH DILLER

Diller Scofidio + Renfro

Diller (b. 1954) co-founded the New York-based practice of Diller Scofidio + Renfro in 1981. Her work spans the fields of architecture, urban design, installation art, multimedia performance and publications, with an emphasis on cultural and civic projects. She is responsible for some of the most renowned buildings of the last decade, including The Broad (opposite) and the High Line in New York (2014). A temporary pavilion on Lake Neuchâtel (below), which was created for the Swiss Expo 2002, is described as an 'architecture of atmosphere'. Diller is professor of architecture at Princeton University.

↓   Blur Building, Yverdon-les-Bains, Switzerland, 2002
→   The Broad, Los Angeles, California, USA, 2015

JANE DREW

Fry, Drew and Partners

Drew (1911–96) was one of Britain's most accomplished and well-known Modernist architects. In the 1950s, she co-founded Fry, Drew and Partners with Maxwell Fry. The practice had a string of important post-war commissions in Britain, including the Pilkington Brothers Head Office (below). Drew and Fry were key figures in the development of the Modernist city of Chandigarh, India, and worked in West Africa designing schools and universities. Drew was created DBE (Dame Commander of the Order of the British Empire) in 1996.

Pilkington Brothers Head Office, St Helens, England, UK, 1964

RAY EAMES

Ray Eames (1912–88) was an enormously influential American designer who created some of the world's best-known architecture, furniture, textiles, graphics and industrial design. She met Charles Eames during her studies at Cranbrook Academy in Michigan, USA, and the duo's collaborative practice became one of the most prolific of the twentieth century. For its identifiable aesthetic out of such practical construction the Eames House (below) – also known as the Case Study House No. 8 – has an enduring place in the canon of great architectural works.

Eames House, Los Angeles, California, USA, 1949, with Charles Eames

JUDITH EDELMAN

Edelman Sultan Knox Wood / Architects

American Modernist architect Edelman (1923–2014) was a pioneering force for change in an era when chances for women in architecture were limited. She graduated from Columbia University in 1946, and set up her own practice in 1960 with Harold Edelman and Stanley Salzman. The firm designed more than 1,500 apartment units and shopping centres, and the Sinai Reform Temple (below), a neo-expressionist synagogue. In 1972, she became the first woman to be elected to the executive committee of the New York chapter of the American Institute of Architects.

Sinai Reform Temple, Bay Shore, New York, USA, 1964

JULIE EIZENBERG

Koning Eizenberg Architecture

Eizenberg (b. 1964) is a founding principal of Koning Eizenberg Architecture, a Los Angeles-based practice set up in 1981. The 28th Street Apartments (below), a restoration and expansion of an existing YMCA building to accommodate supportive housing and invigorating social spaces, is among the firm's many projects that pursue humanist values. The firm was named American Institute of Architects' 2009 California Firm of the Year – one of more than 150 awards won by Koning Eizenberg.

28th Street Apartments, Los Angeles, California, USA, 2012

SOFÍA VON ELLRICHSHAUSEN

Pezo von Ellrichshausen

Von Ellrichshausen (b. 1976) founded Chile-based studio Pezo von Ellrichshausen with Mauricio Pezo in 2002. The practice marries art and architecture, and their buildings utilize unusual, elegant forms and are carefully crafted. The firm's work has been exhibited at various institutions – including the Royal Academy of Arts in London and the Art Institute of Chicago. Von Ellrichshausen has lectured widely and holds the position of design critic in Architecture at Harvard University Graduate School of Design.

↓   Rode House, Chiloé Island, Chile, 2017

FRIDA ESCOBEDO

Escobedo (b. 1979) studied architecture at the Ibero-American University in her home town of Mexico City, then took a master's degree in art, design and the public domain at Harvard in the US. She founded her own practice in 2006, and is celebrated for restoring urban spaces and for using simple materials and forms. In 2018, Escobedo became the youngest architect to work on the Serpentine Pavilion (opposite, top). Other projects include the restoration of La Tallera, the former home and studio of painter David Alfaro Siqueiros (opposite, bottom), one of Mexico's most important art spaces.

→   Serpentine Pavilion, London, England, UK, 2018
↘   La Tallera, Cuernavaca, Mexico, 2010

GABRIELA ETCHEGARAY

Ambrosi I Etchegaray

Etchegaray (b. 1984) was born in Mexico City, and studied architecture and urbanism at the Ibero-American University, from which she graduated in 2008. She explored the arenas of art and jewellery in subsequent studies and work, integrating the disciplines into architectural assignments. In 2011, she established Ambrosi | Etchegaray in Mexico City with Jorge Ambrosi. Their projects include the Mexican Pavilion, 'Echoes of a Land', at the 2018 Venice Architecture Biennale and IT Building (opposite), an apartment complex with an exposed concrete frame.

← IT Building, Mexico City, Mexico, 2016

INGER AUGUSTA EXNER

Inger Augusta Exner (b. 1926) was a leading light in twentieth-century Danish religious architecture, and designed dozens of churches in collaboration with Johannes Exner. She graduated from the Royal Danish Academy of Fine Arts in 1954, and set up her own practice, with Johannes, in Aarhus in 1958. The duo were known for projects such as the Islev Church (below), Gug Church in Aalborg (1973) and the restoration of Koldinghus Castle (1992), Denmark, which earned them the Europa Nostra Award in 1994. In 1983, they were awarded the Eckersberg Medal and, in 1991, the Nykredit Architecture Prize.

↓ Islev Church, Rødovre, Denmark, 1969

YVONNE FARRELL AND SHELLEY MCNAMARA

Grafton Architects

Farrell (b. 1951) and McNamara (b. 1952) studied together at University College Dublin (UCD) and set up their practice – named after the central Dublin street where they first had their office – in 1978. Grafton has come to specialize in impactful large-scale public buildings. As both practitioners and teachers (at UCD, Harvard and Yale, among others), and through their curation of the Venice Architecture Biennale in 2018, the duo have influenced a generation of architects with their principled and ethical approach to the built environment.

↓   School of Economics, Università Luigi Bocconi, Milan, Italy, 2008
→   University Campus UTEC, Lima, Peru, 2015

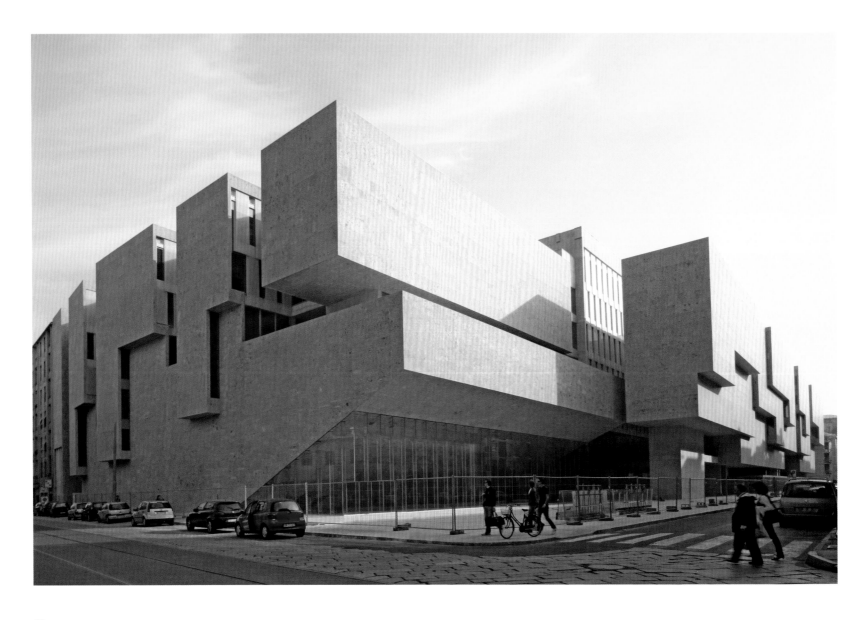

IF A WOMAN IS CONSIDERABLY BETTER AND MORE PRODUCTIVE THAN HER MALE COUNTERPART, SHE CAN RISE CLOSE TO THE TOP.

Norma Merrick Sklarek

OLGA FELIP

Arquitecturia

Felip (b. 1980) was born in Girona, Spain, and graduated from the Barcelona School of Architecture in 2005, where her teachers included Carme Pigem (p. 150). Felip founded the practice Arquitecturia with Josep Camps in 2006, the duo seeking to reinvent traditional Catalan built culture in a contemporary way. Arquitecturia represented Catalonia at the Venice Architecture Biennale in 2012 and the following year Felip won the Moira Gemmill Prize for Emerging Architecture from the Women in Architecture awards.

Ferreries Cultural Centre, Ferreries, Menorca, Spain, 2013

KATHRYN FINDLAY

Ushida Findlay Architects

Findlay (1953–2014) was born in Scotland but made her name as an avant-garde Modernist architect in Japan. She moved to Tokyo in 1979, after graduating from the Architectural Association School in London. There she established Ushida Findlay Architects with Eisaku Ushida. The duo created brilliantly original projects such as the Soft and Hairy House (1994) and the Truss Wall House (below), both in Tokyo. Findlay moved back to the UK in 1999, and collaborated with Anish Kapoor on the ArcelorMittal Orbit tower in the Queen Elizabeth Olympic Park, London (2012).

Truss Wall House, Tokyo, Japan, 1993

WENDY FOSTER

Team 4

British architectural studio Team 4 (1963–7) comprised
Wendy Foster (1937–89), Su Rogers (p. 161), Richard
Rogers and Norman Foster. The firm's heritage-listed,
lakeside Creek Vean House (below) is constructed
predominantly from concrete blocks that are worked
to an extraordinary level of precision. It was the first
ever house to win a Royal Institute of British Architects
Award. Wendy went on to establish Foster Associates
with Norman, where she was involved in large-scale
buildings such as the Sainsbury Centre for Visual Arts
in Norwich (1978) and the Hong Kong and Shanghai
Bank building in Hong Kong (1985).

Creek Vean House, Feock, England, UK, 1966

JEANNE GANG

Studio Gang

Gang (b. 1964) leads architecture and urban design practice Studio Gang. Founded in Chicago in 1997, her studio's research-based design process is centered on advancing social and environmental issues across scales and typologies. Her award-winning body of work includes cultural centres that convene diverse audiences; public and civic projects that connect citizens with ecology; exhibitions that challenge material properties; and high-rise towers that foster a sense of community. A MacArthur Fellow, Gang was the only architect included on *Time* magazine's list of the 100 most influential people of 2019. She is the author of three books and a professor in practice at the Harvard Graduate School of Design, her alma mater.

↓   Eleanor Boathouse at Park 571, Chicago, Illinois, USA, 2016
→   Writers Theatre, Glencoe, Illinois, USA, 2016

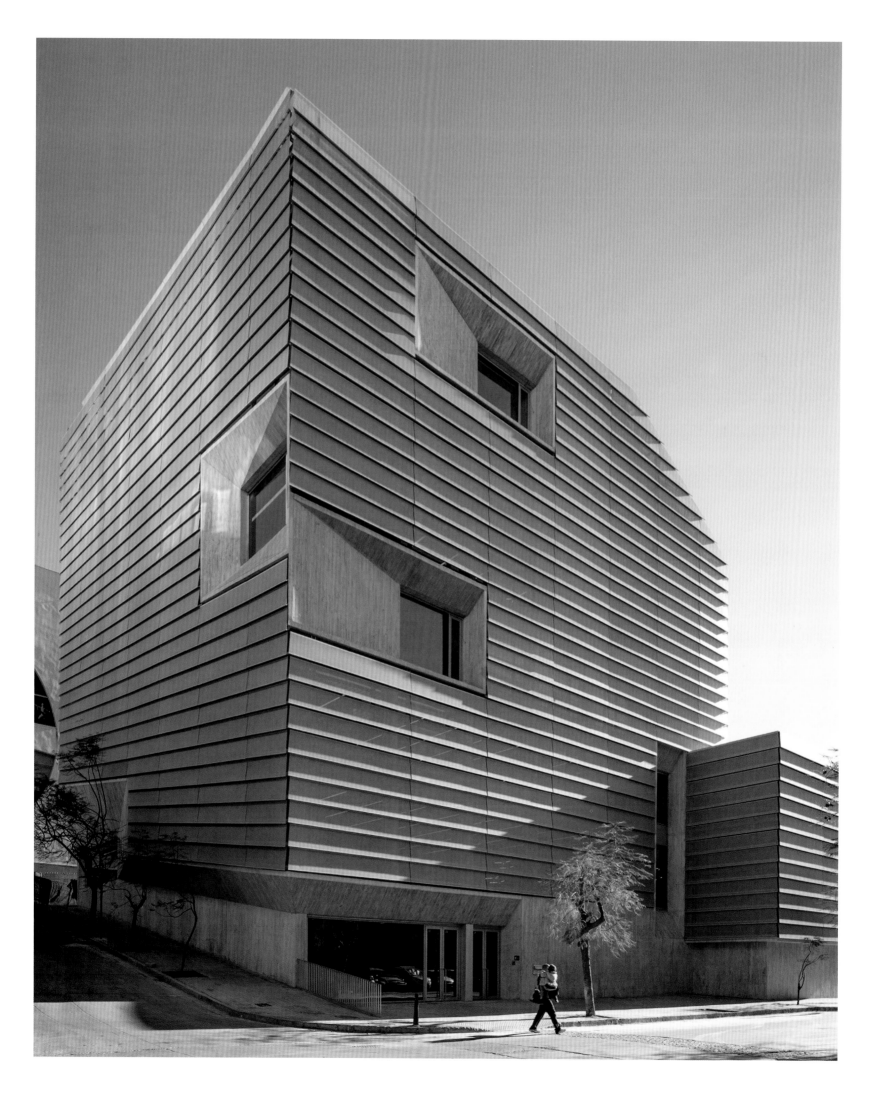

ÁNGELA GARCÍA DE PAREDES

Paredes Pedrosa Architects

García de Paredes (b. 1958) graduated from the Superior Technical School of Architecture of Madrid in 1983, and co-founded Paredes Pedrosa in Madrid in 1990 with Ignacio Pedrosa. Their built work includes numerous heritage interventions, such as Roman Villa La Olmeda (2009), Ceuta Public Library (opposite) and Twin Houses in Oropesa (2015). The duo has won many awards, notably the Spanish Government's Fine Arts Gold Medal in 2014. They are professors at the Madrid School of Architecture as well as in Pamplona, Barcelona and Venice.

← Public Library in Ceuta, Spain, 2013

MANUELLE GAUTRAND

Manuelle Gautrand Architecture

French architect Gautrand (b. 1961) graduated from the École Nationale Supérieure d'Architecture in Montpellier, France, in 1985. She established her own practice in Lyons in 1991 with Marc Blaising, moving to Paris three years later to work on a wide range of projects – notably, the Citroën C42 showroom on the Champs-Élysées (2007) and The Forum (below), a cultural, sport and community centre. She was named as the 2017 laureate of the European Prize for Architecture – the first woman (and the first French architect) to receive the honour.

↓ The Forum, Saint-Louis, France, 2015

LINA GHOTMEH

Lina Ghotmeh — Architecture

Ghotmeh (b. 1980) was born in Beirut, where she studied at the American University, and then taught at the École Spéciale d'Architecture in Paris between 2008 and 2015. In 2005, while working in London and collaborating with Ateliers Jean Nouvel and Foster + Partners, she won a competition to design the Estonian National Museum (below) – after which she established her own studio. Her practice is driven by a desire to connect with people and the natural world. Ghotmeh was nominated for the Moira Gemmill Prize for Emerging Architecture from the Women in Architecture awards in 2019.

Estonian National Museum, Tartu, Estonia, 2016

RATHER THAN TRYING TO KICK THE ESTABLISHMENT WALLS DOWN, WE'RE WALKING IN THROUGH THE FRONT DOOR.

Elizabeth Diller

SARA DE GILES

Morales de Giles Architects

De Giles (n.d.) graduated from the School of
Architecture, Seville, in 1998, and in the same
year joined José Morales to form Morales de Giles
Architects. De Giles has been honoured with a
number of national and international awards, and
her work has been exhibited at numerous Venice
Architecture Biennales, as well as in the exhibition
On-Site: New Architecture in Spain at the Museum
of Modern Art (MoMA) in New York in 2006. The firm's
use of intermediary spaces in their work presents
a modern take on Andalusian architectural traditions.

Níjar Theater, Almería, Spain, 2007

PETRA GIPP

Petra Gipp Arkitektur

Gipp (b. 1967) is a Swedish architect who studied at the Academy of Fine Arts in Copenhagen, Denmark, and founded her own practice, Petra Gipp Arkitektur, in Stockholm in 2009. Among the practice's honours are the 2011 Skåne Architecture Award and the 2015 Wan Future Projects Residential Award. The firm was also nominated for a Mies van der Rohe Award in 2015 for The Cathedral (below); the structure, described as a workshop for audio-visual design, is credited with having sheer clarity of plan and vision.

The Cathedral, Linköping, Sweden, 2014

SILVIA GMÜR

Silvia Gmür Reto Gmür Architekten

Gmür (b. 1939) is a Swiss architect who worked in Paris, London and New York before establishing her own practice in Basel, Switzerland, in 1972. Her notable projects include a concrete villa on Lake Maggiore (below), the renovation of the historic Engelhof building for the University of Basel (1986–90), and her work on public healthcare buildings. Gmür was awarded the Swiss Government's Prix Meret Oppenheim for achievement in art and architecture in 2001, and was president of the Federation of Swiss Architects between 2002 and 2005.

Casa ai Pozzi, Minusio, Switzerland, 2011

JADWIGA GRABOWSKA-HAWRYLAK

Considered to be one of the most important Polish Modernist architects, Grabowska-Hawrylak (1920–2018) spent much of her life in Wrocław, after graduating from the city's University of Technology in 1950. She played a leading role in rebuilding Poland after World War II, working on ruined houses that had to be restored to their original state. She made a name for herself on the iconic Grunwaldzki Square housing complex (opposite), which is popularly referred to as 'Manhattan'. Grabowska-Hawrylak is also remembered for her designs for the quiltwork that she carried out in later life.

← Grunwaldzki Square, Wrocław, Poland, 1973

MARIA GIUSEPPINA GRASSO CANNIZZO

Italian architect Grasso Cannizzo (b. 1952) was born in Sicily and subsequently studied at the University of Rome, where she taught from 1974 to 1980. She then worked in Turin, alongside innovative artists such as Mario Merz and Alighiero Boetti, as well as gaining industrial design experience at Fiat. Today, her practice creates small-scale but complex projects in Sicily – such as FCN 2009 (below), a holiday house, which won the 2012 Royal Institute of British Architects Award. Grasso Cannizzo was also awarded the prestigious 2012 Gold Medal by the Triennale di Milano.

↓ FCN 2009, Sicily, Italy, 2011

EILEEN GRAY

Irish-born architect and designer Gray (1878–1976) settled in Paris in 1902 and became a leading figure in the French decorative arts throughout the 1910s and 20s. Her highly innovative chrome, steel-tube and glass furniture influenced a number of renowned designers of the period, including Charlotte Perriand (p. 148), Le Corbusier, Marcel Breuer and Mies van der Rohe. Though Gray built very little, realizing only nine buildings in her lifetime, her best-known work – Villa E-1027 on the sea in Roquebrune-Cap-Martin (below) – is an iconic work of early Modernist architecture.

Villa E-1027, Roquebrune-Cap-Martin, France, 1929

ZAHA HADID

Zaha Hadid Architects

Hadid (1950–2016) was an Iraqi-born, UK-based architect and one of the most influential practitioners of her generation, with a portfolio of landmark buildings around the world. A trailblazer, she has been described as having 'unmoored contemporary architecture from its affinities for right angles and male dominance', and her practice is best known for its embrace of parametricism. She was the first woman to win the Pritzker Prize in 2004 and received the UK's most important architectural award, the Stirling Prize, in 2010 and 2011. In 2015 she became the first and only woman to be awarded the Royal Gold Medal for Architecture by the Royal Institute of British Architects.

↓   Phaeno Science Centre, Wolfsburg, Germany, 2005
↓↓ Heydar Aliyev Center, Baku, Azerbaijan, 2013

ZOFIA HANSEN

Hansen (1924–2013) graduated from the Faculty of Architecture at Warsaw University of Technology and was the co-creator – with Oskar Hansen – of Open Form theory, an important school of thought in Polish architecture. According to Open Form, architecture should be created with the end user in mind, rather than (as Hansen interpreted Modernism) as a closed art form in which the user had no choice. The transformability of their private house (below) is an embodiment of the concept.

↓   House in Szumin, Poland, 1968

MOJGAN AND GISUE HARIRI

Hariri & Hariri Architecture

Mojgan (b. 1958) and Gisue (b. 1956) left their home country of Iran in the 1970s to study at Cornell University in the USA. They set up Hariri & Hariri Architecture in New York in 1986, working on a wide range of projects from luxury hotels to single-family homes, as well as furniture, jewellery and other product design. They create imaginative buildings, such as Jewels of Salzburg in Austria (2014) and Alvand Tower in Tehran (opposite). The practice won the Academy Award in Architecture at the American Academy of Arts and Letters Awards in 2005.

→   Alvand Tower, Tehran, Iran, 2016

ITSUKO HASEGAWA

Itsuko Hasegawa Atelier

Hasegawa (b. 1941) is one of Japan's most important architects. She became the first winner of the Royal Academy of Arts' Architecture Prize in 2018, with the jury claiming that her 'buildings exude an optimism that could be interpreted as utopianism'. Hasegawa started her career working with Japan's Metabolist group of architects and then collaborated with Kazuo Shinohara. She set up her own practice in Tokyo in 1979, and became the first woman architect to design a public building in Japan with the Shonandai Cultural Centre in Fujisawa (1990), conceived as a reduced model of the universe. The Yamanashi Museum of Fruit (below) consists of three delicate, futuristic domes.

↓   Yamanashi Museum of Fruit, Ezohara, Yamanashi
    Prefecture, Japan, 1994

RÓISÍN HENEGHAN

Heneghan Peng Architects

Heneghan (b. 1963) was born in the Republic of Ireland, where she studied at University College Dublin. She completed her master's degree at Harvard in the US and co-founded Heneghan Peng Architects with Shih-Fu Peng in New York in 1999, the duo moving to a Dublin office two years later. Their work includes the Giant's Causeway Visitors' Centre in Northern Ireland (2012), which was shortlisted for the 2013 Stirling Prize. Faceted structures are a Heneghan Peng hallmark, as seen in the Museum Tonofenfabrik (opposite), which updates an existing industrial building. Heneghan was shortlisted for the 2012 Architect of the Year prize in the Women in Architecture awards.

→   Museum Tonofenfabrik, Lahr, Germany, 2018

ANNA HERINGER

Studio Anna Heringer

German architect Heringer (b. 1977) graduated from the University of Arts and Industrial Design in Linz, Austria, in 2004. Early in her career, she spent a year in Bangladesh where she developed an interest in creating sustainable and humane spaces using natural building materials. Her work has been shown at the Museum of Modern Art (MoMA) in New York as well as the 2010 Venice Architecture Biennale. Heringer won the Aga Khan Award for Architecture in 2007 and the Global Award for Sustainable Architecture in 2011.

METI Handmade School, Rudrapur, Bangladesh, 2006

MARGARETHE
HEUBACHER-SENTOBE

Austrian architect Heubacher-Sentobe (b. 1945)
studied at the Academy of Fine Arts in Vienna, under
the tutelage of Roland Rainer, before working at Loch,
Tuscher and Norer in Innsbruck, establishing her
own practice in Schwaz in 1978. She is best known
for her design of the Carmelite Convent of St Joseph
and St Teresa in Innsbruck (2003), although she
also specializes in unusual family homes like Haus L
(below). Among Heubacher-Sentobe's honours are
the 1999 New Building in the Alps Award and the 2016
Tyrolean Medal of Merit. She taught design at the
University of Innsbruck from 1990 until 2011.

Haus L, Weerberg, Austria, 1996

MIMI HOANG

nARCHITECTS

Hoang (b. 1971) studied at the Massachusetts Institute of Technology and Harvard in the US, then worked in New York, Boston and Amsterdam. She co-founded nARCHITECTS in 1999 with Eric Bunge. The practice made an impact with Carmel Place, New York's first micro-unit apartment building (2016), and Chicago Navy Pier, the centrepiece of which is the curvilinear Wave Wall (below), sheathed in louvres. Hoang has also taught widely, and is a professor at Columbia University.

Chicago Navy Pier, Chicago, Illinois, USA, 2016, with James Corner Field Operations

SAIJA HOLLMÉN, JENNI REUTER AND HELENA SANDMAN

Hollmén Reuter Sandman Architects

Architects Hollmén (b. 1970), Reuter (b. 1972) and Sandman (b. 1972) started their collaboration in 1995 with the Women's Centre project in Senegal (2001). From a base in Finland, their projects include interiors, architecture and urban planning. All three teach at Aalto University in Otaniemi. Presentations for three community-based design projects, including the KWIECO Shelter House (below), were exhibited at the 2016 Venice Architecture Biennale.

KWIECO Shelter House, Moshi, Tanzania, from 2012

BEATE HØLMEBAKK

Manthey Kula Arkitekter

Hølmebakk (b. 1963) graduated from the Oslo School of Architecture, Norway, where she is now a professor, in 1990. She established Manthey Kula in 2004 with Per Tamsen, and together they explore architecture's relationship with art and the landscape. The studio's projects include the Pålsbu Hydro Power Station (2007), recognized for its complex and unexpected geometry, and the sculptural Forvik Ferry Port (below), a massive inverted barrel vault structure. Hølmebakk was the recipient of an honorary medal from the Erich Schelling Architecture Foundation.

Forvik Ferry Terminal, Helgeland, Norway, 2015

PATTY HOPKINS

Hopkins Architects

Patty Hopkins (b. 1942) won the Royal Gold Medal
for Architecture from the Royal Institute of British
Architects, along with Sir Michael Hopkins, in 1994.
Patty set up her own practice after graduating
from London's Architectural Association School in
1968, but then joined forces with Michael in 1976
as Hopkins Architects. The duo promoted the use
of lightweight, often prefabricated materials; open
and flexible interiors; and exposed steel structures –
features epitomized in the Hopkins House (below),
and associated with the High-Tech movement
in architecture.

Hopkins House, London, England, UK, 1976

NAOKO HORIBE

Horibe Associates

Japanese architect Horibe (b. 1972) graduated from Kinki University (now called Kindai University) in 1995, and worked for major architectural firm Takenaka. She set up her own practice, Horibe Associates, in Osaka in 2003. She has designed many buildings – such as the White Rose English School (below) and the House in Mayu (2013) in Kishiwada, Japan – driven by the long-term impact that her work will have on the local environment. Horibe teaches at her former university, and is a member of the Japan Institute of Architects.

↓   White Rose English School, Takatsuki, Osaka
    Prefecture, Japan, 2014

FRANCINE HOUBEN

Mecanoo Architecten

Dutch architect Houben (b. 1955) published her seminal manifesto *Composition, Contrast, Complexity* in 2001, and was curator of the first International Architecture Biennale Rotterdam two years later, bringing the theme of the aesthetics of mobility to the forefront of international design consciousness. In 2010 Houben was granted lifelong membership of the Akademie der Künste in Berlin and in 2015 she was presented the Prins Bernhard Cultuurfonds Prize by Queen Máxima of the Netherlands for her oeuvre, which includes many award-winning libraries.

→   Kaap Skil, Maritime and Beachcombers Museum,
    Texel, Netherlands, 2011
↘   Library of Birmingham, England, UK, 2013

I WAS TOLD GIRLS DON'T GO TO TECHNICAL UNIVERSITIES.

Itsuko Hasegawa

ROSSANA HU

Neri & Hu

Hu (n.d.) studied at Princeton and the University of California, both in the US, before co-founding Neri & Hu Design and Research Office with Lyndon Neri in 2004. The firm, based in Shanghai and London, is now one of China's foremost architecture and design practices. Their work has a clean simplicity, as seen in the Suzhou Chapel (below). Neri & Hu's work has been recognized by a number of prestigious awards, including Designer of the Year by *Wallpaper** in 2014.

Suzhou Chapel, Suzhou, Jiangsu Province, China, 2016

HUANG WENJING

Open Architecture

Chinese architect Huang Wenjing (b. 1973) graduated from Beijing's Tsinghua University in 1996, followed by a master's degree at Princeton three years later. She set up Open Architecture in 2003 with co-founder Li Hu, which has offices in New York and Beijing. Their striking projects include Tank Shanghai (2019), an art museum and cultural centre, and the UCCA Dune Art Museum (below), built into a sand dune near the Chinese coastal city of Qinhuangdao. Huang also holds a professorial position at the University of Hong Kong.

↓   UCCA Dune Art Museum, Qinhuangdao, Hebei
    Province, China, 2018, with Li Hu

LOUISA HUTTON

Sauerbruch Hutton

Hutton (b. 1957) was born in Norwich, UK, and studied at Bristol University and the Architectural Association School in London. She worked with Alison and Peter Smithson (p. 181) for four years before setting up in business with Matthias Sauerbruch in London in 1989. Sauerbruch Hutton moved to Berlin in 1993, and their projects – often colourful, angular and sensual – include the GSW Headquarters (opposite) and the M9 Museum District (2018) in Venice-Mestre, Italy. The firm has won several Royal Institute of British Architects and American Institute of Architects awards.

→   GSW Headquarters, Berlin, Germany, 1999

ELEENA JAMIL

Eleena Jamil Architect

Jamil (b. 1971) graduated from the Welsh School of Architecture at Cardiff University, UK, and is the principal of Eleena Jamil Architect (EJA). The studio was formed in 2005 in Kuala Lumpur, and favours the use of sustainable, locally sourced material – often bamboo – and labour. EJA projects include the Buzz.ar community centre (2019) and the Bamboo Playhouse public pavilion (below) – both in the Malaysian capital. EJA was shortlisted for *Dezeen*'s 2018 Architect of the Year Award and the 2017 Firm of the Year Award for Sustainable Architecture by the American Architecture Prize.

Bamboo Playhouse, Kuala Lumpur, Malaysia, 2015

EVA JIŘIČNÁ

Influential architect Jiřičná (b. 1939) was born in what was then Czechoslovakia and studied architecture and engineering at the Prague Academy of Fine Arts, graduating in 1962. She moved to the UK in 1968 and established her own practice, marrying her architectural and engineering experience to great effect. Her interior design projects are particularly well known, including the early clothes shops for Joseph (1980s) and Lloyd's of London (1986). Jiřičná has been honoured by the British and Czech governments as well as by the Royal Academy of Arts in the UK.

Cultural and Congress Centre, Zlín, Czech Republic, 2011

SHARON JOHNSTON

Johnston Marklee

Johnston (n.d.) co-founded the Los Angeles-based firm Johnston Marklee with Mark Lee in 1998. Their buildings are diverse in scale and type, and have been described as operating at both the experiential and the intellectual level. They are also recognized for their interesting residential projects, five of which are presented in the monograph *House Is A House Is A House Is A House Is A House* (2012). They were the joint artistic directors of the 2017 Chicago Architecture Biennial.

←   Vault House, Pacific Palisades, California, USA, 2004
↙   View House, Rosário, Argentina, 2009

CARLA JUAÇABA

Brazilian architect Juaçaba (b. 1976) set up her practice in 2000 after graduating from Universidade Santa Úrsula in Rio de Janeiro. Juaçaba's projects span from private residences to an outdoor chapel structure designed for the 2018 Vatican contribution to the Venice Architecture Biennale and an exhibit hall for Rio+20 (below). Her work has been praised for its consistency and continuity. She has lectured at Harvard and Columbia University in the US and was winner of the Moira Gemmill Prize for Emerging Architecture from the Women in Architecture awards in 2018.

↓   Pavilion Humanidade, Rio de Janeiro, Brazil, 2012

MOMOYO KAIJIMA

Atelier Bow-Wow

Japanese architect Kaijima (b. 1969) graduated from
the Japan Women's University in 1991, and then
received a master's degree in engineering at the Tokyo
Institute of Technology in 1994. She established Atelier
Bow-Wow with Yoshiharu Tsukamoto in 1992. Their
design philosophy, which they call 'behaviourology',
is centred on the various behaviours of three things –
natural elements, human beings and the building itself
– and their architecture is known for being imbued
with a quirky humour. Kaijima is a professor at the
University of Tsukuba in Japan, and has taught widely.

Four Boxes Gallery, Skive, Denmark, 2009

MARIAM KAMARA

Atelier Masōmī

Kamara (b. 1979) was born in Niger, graduated from Purdue University in Indiana, USA, then received a master's degree at the University of Washington. In 2013, she co-founded united4design, a Seattle-based architects' collective that works in the US, Afghanistan and Niger. A year later, she established her own practice, Atelier Masōmī, where she works on a wide range of cultural and educational projects in the developing world. British architect Sir David Adjaye selected Kamara to be his protégé in 2018 under the Rolex Arts Initiative.

Hikma Religious and Secular Complex, Dandaji, Niger, 2018, with Studio Chahar

ILSE MARIA KÖNIGS

Königs Architekten

Königs (b. 1962) was born in Austria and graduated
from Innsbruck University in 1990. She then moved
to Cologne, where she spent time working with
German architects Joachim Schürmann and Peter
Kulka, before co-founding Königs Architekten in 1996
with Ulrich Königs. The practice is best known for its
'Church by the Sea' (below), clad in a dark Oldenburg
brick, and for its uncompromisingly modern design
of the St Francis Parish Centre in Regensburg (2004),
which was nominated for the 2005 European Union
Mies van der Rohe Award.

St Marien, Schillig, Germany, 2012

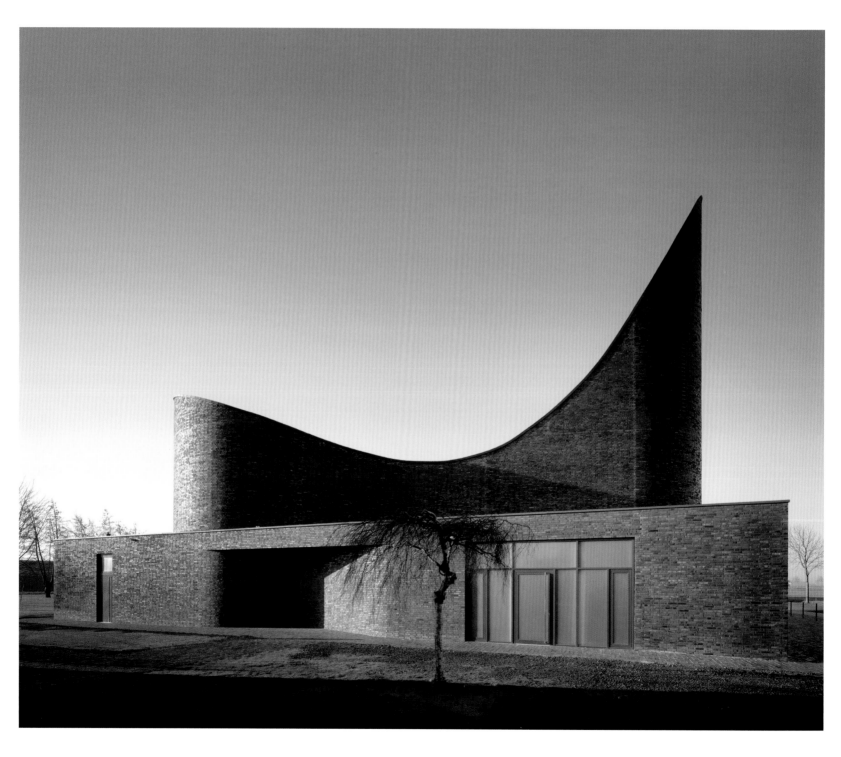

EVA KOPPEL

KKET

Eva Koppel (1916–2006) ran one of Denmark's most important architectural studios, KKET, with Nils Koppel. She was born in Copenhagen and graduated from the city's Danish Academy in 1941. She and Nils worked in Alvar Aalto's studio before setting up their own practice in 1946. They gained a reputation for large projects designed in the Brutalist style, notably the Langelinie Pavilion (1957), the Technical University of Denmark in Lundtofte (1975) and the Panum Building (below). KKET won the prestigious Eckersberg Medal in 1955, awarded by the Royal Danish Academy of the Arts.

Panum Building, Copenhagen, Denmark, 1986

MARGARET KROPHOLLER

Kropholler (1891–1966) was the first professional female architect in the Netherlands. She joined her brother's architectural practice in 1907 while also studying at the Amsterdam Academy of Architecture. The evocative House VI (below) is one of seventeen houses within the artists' colony of Park Meerwijk, one of the first Dutch Expressionist projects. Kropholler received international recognition in 1925 when she was awarded the silver medal at the Paris Decorative Arts Exhibition. Her work later became more Modernist in approach, and she collaborated with the Dutch architect Jan Frederik Staal on the Beurs-World Trade Centre in Rotterdam (1940).

House VI, Bergen, The Netherlands, 1918

ANUPAMA KUNDOO

Anupama Kundoo Architects

Kundoo (b. 1967) established herself as an architect in Auroville, in southern India, where her research-focussed approach to architecture was developed. The Wall House (below) demonstrates her experimentation in low-impact building technologies that are socio-economically and environmentally beneficial. Kundoo studied for her doctoral degree at the Technical University of Berlin in 2008, then moved to Australia in 2011, where she was a senior lecturer at the University of Queensland, and then to Europe in 2014, where she teaches at the Camilo José Cela University in Madrid.

Wall House, Auroville, India, 2000

ANNE LACATON

Lacaton & Vassal

Lacaton (b. 1955) earned a master's degree in urban planning at the University of Bordeaux in 1984. She has maintained her involvement in academia, with professorial roles in Europe and the US. She formed her own practice with Jean-Philippe Vassal in 1989. The Lacaton & Vassal approach ensures that the individual human experience is paramount. Her mantra is 'Transform, add, reuse, never demolish!' The firm creates unusual but modest projects, such as their house in the Dordogne (below), in which the structure's metallic cladding gives an almost magical presence to the otherwise simple form.

House, Dordogne, France, 1997

ANNABEL LAHZ

lahznimmo architects

Lahz (b. 1963) graduated from the University of Queensland in the 1980s and, together with Andrew Nimmo, established lahznimmo architects in 1994 in Sydney. The philosophy of the practice is underpinned by a desire to de-emphasize the role of the individual and focus on collaboration. Specializing in public and community projects, including the Centennial Park Amenities (below) and Bowen Place Crossing (2015), the studio is celebrated for its ideas-based approach and interest in the relationship between landscape, urban design and architecture.

Centennial Park Amenities, Sydney, NSW, Australia, 2006

ANOUK LEGENDRE

XTU

Legendre (b. 1962) and Nicolas Desmazières founded XTU in Paris in 2000, specializing in bold residential and cultural buildings, including the bulbous Cité du Vin (below), which houses a wine museum. The firm's architectural work is shaped by the innovative research that it carries out in biotechnology and the effect that living organisms will have on all our lives. Other projects include the Jeongok Prehistory Museum in South Korea (2013) and the French Pavilion at the Milan Expo (2015).

Cité du Vin, Bordeaux, France, 2016

REGINE LEIBINGER

Barkow Leibinger

German architect Leibinger (b. 1963) studied at the
Technical University of Berlin, graduating in 1989, and
Harvard (1991), where she met Frank Barkow. They
founded their own practice, Barkow Leibinger, in 1993,
based in Berlin and New York, with projects covering
all sectors of building types and exhibitions, notably
the partly subterranean Biosphere (below), an indoor
tropical botanical garden, and the Tour Total (2012),
a rippling tower in Berlin. Leibinger has taught at many
institutions, including Princeton University. The firm
has won five National American Institute of Architects
Honor Awards.

Biosphere, Potsdam, Germany, 2001

MAYA LIN

Maya Lin Studio

Lin (b. 1959) was born in Ohio, USA, the niece of Lin Huiyin, the first female architect in modern China. She graduated from Yale University in 1981 and, at the age of twenty-two, she designed the Vietnam Veterans Memorial (below), a controversial project at the time in part for its balancing between art and architecture. An interest in the environment guides her practice, which includes landscape art and public sculpture, as well as large-scale built works. A documentary about her won an Academy Award in 1995, and she was awarded the Presidential Medal of Freedom in 2016.

Vietnam Veterans Memorial, Washington, DC, USA, 1982

NERMA LINSBERGER

Austrian architect Linsberger (n.d.) was born in Sarajevo, Bosnia-Herzegovina (then Yugoslavia), and studied under Timo Pentillä and Massimiliano Fuksas at the Academy of Fine Arts in Vienna. She stayed in the city to work in various architectural practices between 1992 and 2009. In 2010, she founded her eponymous firm and is renowned for her important social housing projects, including Mühlgrund (below) and Sakura (2016), which won the German Design Award in 2018.

Mühlgrund, Vienna, Austria, 2016

JING LIU

SO–IL

Liu (b. 1980) was born in Nanjing, China, and co-founded SO–IL with Dutch architect Florian Idenburg in New York in 2008. The studio creates refined urban spaces, residences and cultural institutions on a variety of scales. Alongside their building works, other projects include Pole Dance (2010), a temporary structure for the PS1 courtyard at the Museum of Modern Art (MoMA) in New York; exhibition design for Meissen porcelain (2011), which consisted of a series of prismatic cases in bright colours; and a furniture system for Knoll (2014).

← Kukje Gallery, Seoul, South Korea, 2012
↙ Jan Shrem and Maria Manetti Shrem Museum of Art, Davis, California, USA, 2016

INÊS LOBO

Inês Lobo Arquitectos

Lobo (b. 1966) graduated from the School of Fine Arts in her home town of Lisbon, Portugal, in 1989, then worked with João Luís Carrilho da Graça and Pedro Domingos before setting up her own practice in 2002. The studio has executed designs for schools, housing projects, cultural institutions and libraries, including the Public Library and Regional Archive of Angra do Heroísmo (below), defined by its clear geometry and open public spaces. She curated the Portuguese Pavilion at the 2012 Venice Architecture Biennale, and in 2014 was named winner of the international arcVision Prize – Women and Architecture.

↓ Public Library and Regional Archive of Angra do Heroísmo, Portugal, 2016

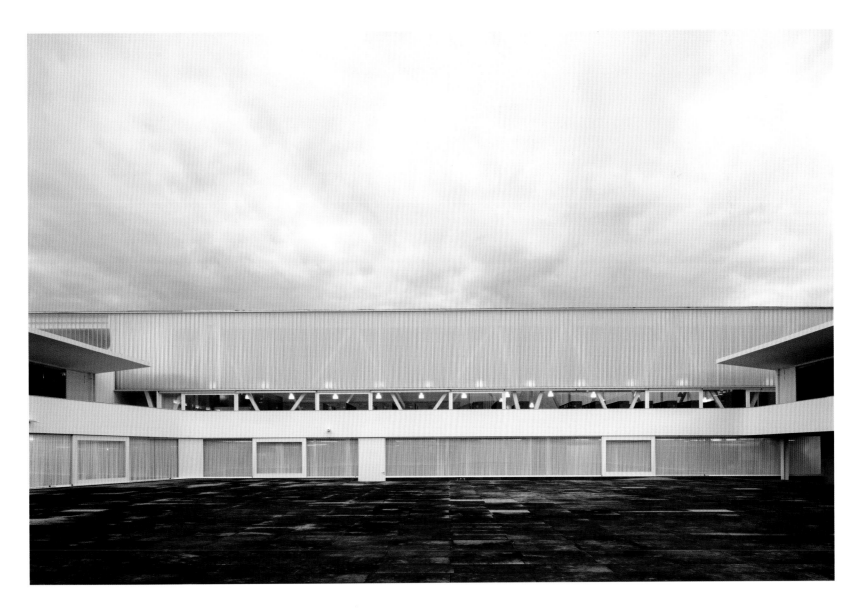

WHAT DO THEY SAY? BEHIND EVERY SUCCESSFUL MAN IS A SURPRISED WOMAN. OR NOW IS IT BEHIND EVERY SUCCESSFUL WOMAN IS AN ANGRY MAN?

Madelon Vriesendorp

MJ LONG

Mary Jane Long (1939–2018), known as MJ Long, was an American architect who studied at Yale in the US before moving to the UK in 1965 to work with Sir Colin St John Wilson, with whom she designed the British Library in London (below). Long spent fifteen years working on the institution, a controversial project while it was being designed and realized. It went on, however, to become the 'youngest' contemporary building to be heritage listed Grade I, the highest level of protection awarded in Britain.

British Library, London, England, UK, 1997

ELLEN VAN LOON

Office for Metropolitan Architecture (OMA)

Dutch architect van Loon (b. 1963) studied architecture in Delft, going on to work with Norman Foster on the reconstruction of the Reichstag in Berlin in the 1990s. She joined Rotterdam-based Office for Metropolitan Architecture (OMA) in 1998, and became a partner in 2002. She has been involved in many large-scale international public projects, including the Casa da Música (below), which won the 2007 Royal Institute of British Architects Award, and the Dutch Embassy in Berlin (2003), which was honoured with an European Union Mies van der Rohe Award in 2005.

Casa da Música, Porto, Portugal, 2005

LU WENYU

Amateur Architecture Studio

Chinese architect Lu Wenyu (b. 1966) studied at
Nanjing Institute of Technology and co-founded
Amateur Architecture Studio in Hangzhou with Wang
Shu in 1997. The firm's name was a rebuke to the
'soulless' architecture that they witnessed in China.
The Ningbo History Museum (below), for example,
uses found materials – including brick, stone and
tile – bound together in concrete using a traditional
technique called *wapan*. Wang Shu alone was
awarded the Pritzker Prize in 2012, however he insisted
that it be shared with Lu Wenyu.

Ningbo History Museum, Ningbo, Zhejiang Province,
China, 2008

STEPHANIE MACDONALD

6a architects

Macdonald (n.d.) established 6a architects with Tom Emerson in 2001. She has since developed the practice's collaborative approach, working with consultants, artists, designers and scientists among others. The studio is best known for its art galleries, educational buildings, artists' studios and residential projects, often in sensitive historic environments. A new building for the MK Gallery (opposite, top) has been described as being poised 'between high technology and low-rise suburbia'. Cowan Court (opposite, bottom) uses oak cladding that echoes the materiality of the original college. The hall of residence won a Royal Institute of British Architects East Award in 2017.

← MK Gallery, Milton Keynes, England, UK, 2019
↙ Cowan Court, Churchill College, University of Cambridge, England, UK, 2017

KATE MACINTOSH

Macintosh (b. 1937) is best known for the social-housing projects that she designed during the 1960s. She was born in Scotland, and graduated from the Edinburgh School of Art in 1961, later working under Denys Lasdun on the Royal National Theatre (1976) in London. Macintosh designed important municipal housing blocks in London and southern England, including Dawson's Heights (below) in Dulwich, in the south of the capital. She established Finch Macintosh Architects with George Finch in 1998, and their Weston Adventure Playground in Southampton won a 2005 Royal Institute of British Architects Award.

↓ Dawson's Heights, London, England, UK, 1972

MARION MAHONY GRIFFIN

American architect Mahony (1871–1961) was an original member, along with Walter Burley Griffin, of the Prairie School of architecture in the Midwest. Rock Crest–Rock Glen (below) is considered the most important urban planning scheme of the style. Mahony worked for fifteen years in the office of Frank Lloyd Wright from 1895, and during that time produced over half of the iconic drawings that helped make Wright famous in Europe. Mahony, with Griffin, went on to work in Australia – notably on designs for the proposed capital of Canberra – and India, in a career that spanned fifty years.

Rock Crest–Rock Glen, Mason City, Iowa, USA, from 1912, with Walter Burley Griffin

DORIANA MANDRELLI FUKSAS

Studio Fuksas

Italian architect and designer Mandrelli Fuksas (b. 1955) graduated from the Sapienza University in Rome in 1979, before attending the École Spéciale d'Architecture in Paris. She began working with Massimiliano Fuksas in 1985 and since 1997 has led the design arm of the practice. Among the studio's most notable projects are the New Church in Foligno (below), a concrete cube; the Zenith Music Hall in Strasbourg (2008), covered with translucent, orange fabric; and an expansion of Shenzhen Bao'an International Airport in China (2013).

New Church in Foligno, São Paulo, Brazil, 2009

DORTE MANDRUP

Mandrup (b. 1961) founded her eponymous Copenhagen-based studio, where she is creative director, in 1999. Her work is characterized as conceptually robust, as well as innovative, not only in terms of form and material, but also by its analytical approach. The Wadden Sea Centre (below) utilizes traditional crafts and materials of the region, seen in its thatched roofs and facades. Mandrup is known for her commitment to the development of the architectural field; she holds visiting professorships abroad and, in 2019, was appointed chair of the Mies van der Rohe Award.

Wadden Sea Centre, Ribe, Denmark, 2017

PAOLA MARANTA

Miller & Maranta

Swiss architect Maranta (b. 1959) studied at the EPFL
(Swiss Federal Institute of Technology) Lausanne and
ETH (Institute of Technology) Zurich, graduating in
1986. She founded Miller & Maranta with Quintus Miller
in 1994, and the duo's approach to architecture is
said to have been influenced by Aldo Rossi's theories
of Analogue Architecture, which they absorbed while
studying in the 1980s. The practice's notable projects
include the concrete Volta School in Basel (2000),
cubic in form, and an open-air market structure (below).

Färberplatz Market Hall, Aarau, Switzerland, 2002

MARY MEDD

Hertfordshire County Architects

Medd (1907–2005) was a leading light of progressive school designers in Britain following World War II, shaped by her upbringing in the planned garden cities of Letchworth and Welwyn. She graduated from the Architectural Association School in London, and a trip to Stockholm in 1930 opened her eyes to Swedish design. She built a group of houses in Hertfordshire (1936), and was hired as the county's first architect. In collaboration with David Medd, she designed schools throughout England. Both Medds were awarded an OBE (Officer of the Order of the British Empire) in 1964.

Alban Wood School, Watford, England, UK, 1954

DÉBORA MESA

Ensamble Studio

Mesa (b. 1981) studied architecture in Madrid before joining Ensamble in 2003, where she was made a partner in 2010. She co-curated the Spanish Pavilion at the Venice Architecture Biennale in 2012 and in the same year founded POPlab (Prototypes of Prefabrication Laboratory) at the Massachusetts Institute of Technology (MIT). Ensamble often work with pre-existing natural conditions to create their projects, such as the Truffle (opposite), which used earth as a temporary mould for the building's form. The Hemeroscopium House (below) is recognized as one of the most unique and idiosyncratic works of architecture of the twenty-first century.

↓   Hemeroscopium House, Las Rozas, Spain, 2008
→   The Truffle, Costa da Morte, Spain, 2010

BELÉN MONEO

Moneo Brock

Spanish architect Moneo (b. 1965) graduated from Harvard in 1988 and co-founded Moneo Brock with Jeffrey Brock in 1993 in New York, opening a Madrid office in 2001. They are firm believers in sustainable architecture that improves quality of life. Composed of steel and glass modules, the multi-use Bosque de Acero pavilion (below) provided infrastructure that acted as a filter between the city and adjacent parkland. Their work also includes the Thermal Baths in Panticosa, Spain (2008), and a striking church in Pueblo Serena, Mexico (2016).

Bosque de Acero, Cuenca, Spain, 2010

JULIA MORGAN

Morgan (1872–1957) was the first woman to earn an architect's licence in California, USA, having graduated from the University of California in 1894, before studying at the École des Beaux-Arts in Paris, France. Morgan opened her own practice in 1904; the San Francisco earthquake of 1906 meant that architects' services were soon in high demand. She built many properties for publishing magnate William Randolph Hearst, including Hearst Castle (opposite). Morgan also became the first woman to receive the Gold Medal from the American Institute of Architects, albeit posthumously, in 2014.

←   Hearst Castle, San Simeon, California, USA, 1947

TOSHIKO MORI

Toshiko Mori Architect

Born in Japan, Mori (b. 1951) has been an innovator within the American architecture scene since she graduated from the School of Architecture at Cooper Union in New York in 1976. She is best known for her public and cultural projects, including THREAD: Artists' Residency and Cultural Centre in Senegal (2015) and the Newspaper Café (below). Mori sits on the board of directors for Architecture of Humanity, a non-profit organization dedicated to design innovations within communities. In 2018 she received the Farnsworth Art Museum's Maine in America Award.

↓   Newspaper Café, Jindong Architecture Park, Jinhua City, Zhejiang Province, China, 2007

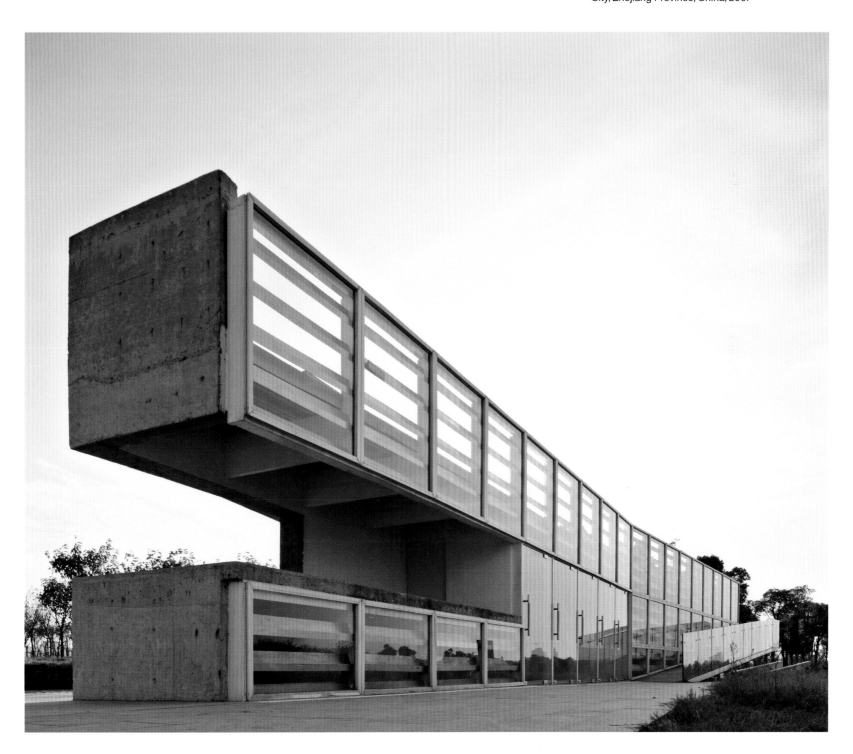

FARSHID MOUSSAVI

Farshid Moussavi Architecture

British architect Moussavi (b. 1965) was born in Iran and co-founded Foreign Office Architects with Alejandro Zaera-Polo in 1993, working on a mixture of projects including the futuristic Yokohama ferry terminal in Japan (below). Moussavi went on to establish Farshid Moussavi Architecture (FMA) in 2011. The studio's projects include the acclaimed MOCA (opposite), clad in mirrored black stainless steel. Moussavi's work is rooted in critical research, which she carries out through FunctionLab, the research branch of FMA.

↓   Yokohama International Passenger Terminal, Yokohama, Kanagawa Prefecture, Japan, 1995
→   Museum of Contemporary Art Cleveland (MOCA), Ohio, USA, 2012

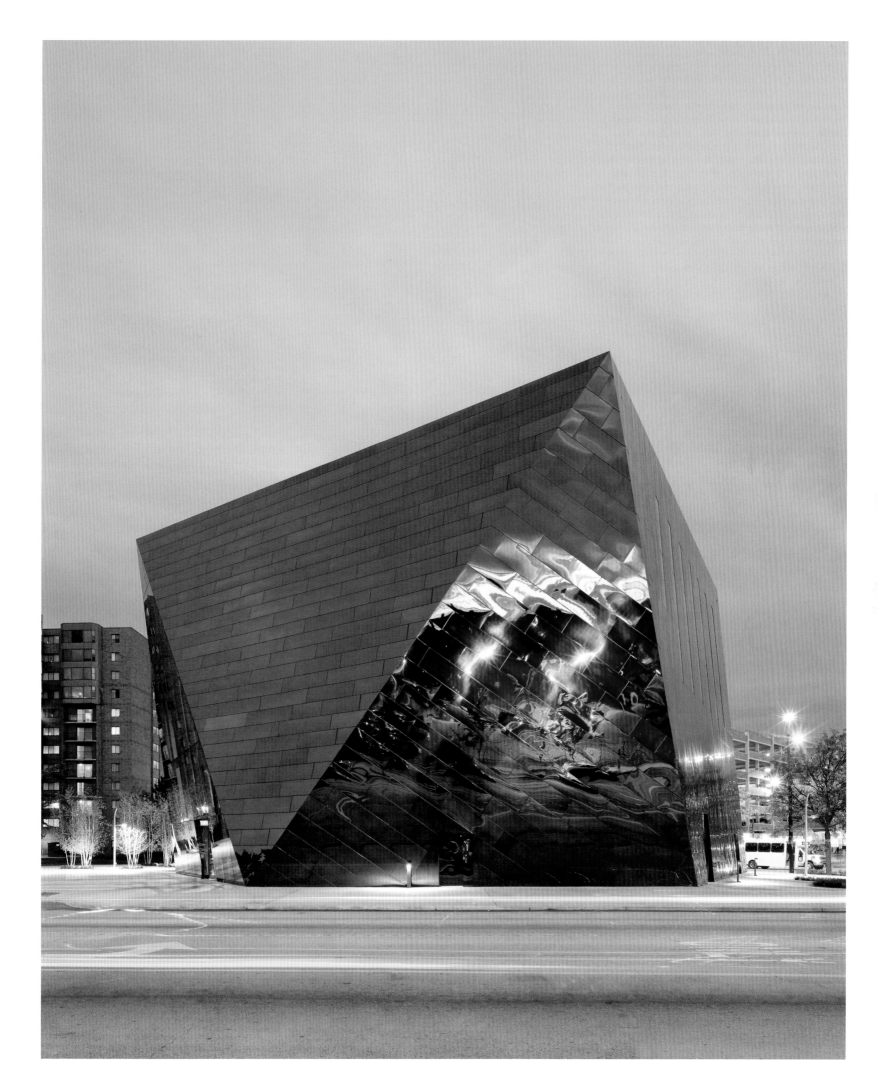

JAKOBA MULDER

Mulder (1900–88) changed the face of her home city while working in Amsterdam's Department of Urban Planning for more than forty years. She joined the municipal department in 1930, succeeding Cornelis van Eesteren as its head in 1958. In the 1930s, she designed Amsterdamse Bos, a new forest sited southwest of the city, creating a park for the benefit of all citizens. She contributed to the city's General Expansion Plan, which was implemented after World War II, and a square in Amsterdam is named in her honour. The neighbourhood of Betondorp (below), experimental at the time, consists of affordable housing made with cheap building materials, chiefly concrete.

Betondorp, Amsterdam, Netherlands, 1925

YUKO NAGAYAMA

Yuko Nagayama & Associates

Nagayama (b. 1975) is a Tokyo-based Japanese architect. She graduated from Showa Women's University in 1998 and went on to found her eponymous practice in 2002 at the age of twenty-six. Nagayama's work includes high-end retail, café and gallery commissions, as well as residential projects, including the Urbanprem Minami Aoyama house (below), with a curved outer wall. She is the recipient of a number of awards, including the Yamanashi Culture Prize for Architecture in 2017 and the Tokyo Architecture Award for Excellence in 2018.

Urbanprem Minami Aoyama, Tokyo, Japan, 2012

IF THE IDEA OF A FEMALE GENDER IS TO BECOME FUEL FOR INNOVATION, THE PRESENCE OF WOMEN IN ARCHITECTURE HAS TO BE LIBERATED FROM THE DIALECTIC OF WOMEN ARCHITECTS VERSUS MEN ARCHITECTS .

Farshid Moussavi

FUENSANTA NIETO

Nieto Sobejano Arquitectos

Nieto (b. 1957) was born in Madrid and studied at the city's Technical University. She co-founded Nieto Sobejano Arquitectos with Enrique Sobejano in 1985, opening a second office in Berlin in 2007. Their major projects include the San Telmo Museum in San Sebastián, Spain (2011), and the underground Interactive Museum of the History of Lugo (below). The studio was the twelfth winner of the Alvar Aalto Medal – and Nieto the first woman to be recognized in the award's forty-eight-year history.

Interactive Museum of the History of Lugo, Spain, 2011

SHEILA O'DONNELL

O'Donnell + Tuomey

O'Donnell (b. 1953) studied at University College Dublin before receiving a master's degree from the Royal College of Art in London in 1980. In 1988, with John Tuomey, she founded O'Donnell + Tuomey. In addition to her practice, O'Donnell has taught and lectured at schools of architecture in Europe, Japan and the US. In 2015, she received the RIBA Royal Gold Medal and the Arnold W. Brunner Memorial Prize – both awarded in recognition of a lifetime's work.

↓   Sean O'Casey Community Centre, Dublin,
    Ireland, 2008
→   LSE Saw Swee Hock Student Centre, London,
    England, UK, 2015

PATRICIA PATKAU

Patkau Architects

Canadian architect Patricia Patkau (b. 1950) graduated from the University of Manitoba in 1973, and received her master's in 1978 from Yale. Along with John Patkau, she established Patkau Architects in 1978, gaining a reputation for a design style that draws on the principles of modern architecture while simultaneously being inspired by the traditions and landscape of the Pacific Northwest. The firm works across various scales and typologies of buildings, from cultural and institutional projects to schools and residences. Patkau is a professor at the University of British Columbia.

↓   Seabird Island School, Agassiz, British Columbia, Canada, 1991
←   Hadaway House, Whistler, British Columbia, Canada, 2013

CHARLOTTE PERRIAND

Perriand (1903–99) is considered one of the most important architects and designers of the twentieth century. She studied in Paris under interior designer Henri Rapin before collaborating with architects Le Corbusier and his cousin Pierre Jeanneret. Among her most iconic furniture pieces is the LC4 Chaise Longue (1930), which Perriand designed while working in the office of Le Corbusier. Perriand strove to improve the quality of life for the users of her designs, and she embraced prefabrication, as is evident in her Modernist, prefab design for Les Arcs (below). Her built work also includes the Air France offices in Brazzaville, Republic of the Congo (c.1952), with Jean Prouvé; and the League of Nations building in Geneva, Switzerland (1957).

Arc 1600, Les Arcs Ski Resort, Savoie, France, 1968

RAILI PIETILÄ

Finnish architect Raili Pietilä (b. 1926) graduated in 1956 from the Helsinki University of Technology, having worked for Olli Kivinen and then Olaf Küttner. In 1966 she established an architectural practice with Reima Pietilä. The duo's notable designs include the Finnish Embassy (below), and a summer cottage on the island of Klovaharun (1965) for Raili's sister, the artist Tuulikki Pietilä, which she famously shared with Tove Jansson, the author of the Moomin books. The Pietiläs's organic approach to Modernism made a huge contribution to twentieth-century Finnish architecture.

Finnish Embassy, New Delhi, India, 1985

CARME PIGEM

RCR Arquitectes

Spanish architect Pigem (b. 1962) established RCR
Arquitectes with Rafael Aranda and Ramón Vilalta
in Olot, Spain, in 1988 – a year after graduating from
the Vallès School of Architecture, where she went
on to work as a professor. She has been a professor
at the ETH (Institute of Technology) Zurich since
2005. The practice is known for its use of weathered
steel, seen in projects such as the Crematorium
Hofheide (below) and De Krook (opposite), the new city
library of Ghent. RCR won the Pritzker Prize in 2017.

↓   Crematorium Hofheide, Holsbeek, Belgium, 2016
→   De Krook Library, Ghent, Belgium, 2017

CARME PINÓS

Estudio Carme Pinós

Pinós (b. 1954) was born in Barcelona, where she set up her own studio in 1991 after winning international recognition for her work with Enric Miralles. Pinós's practice is multifaceted, and includes social housing and urban regeneration as well as furniture design – her philosophy is one of inclusive social interaction with and within her designs. Her home town projects include the ceramic-clad, cantilevering La Massana Fine Arts School (below), but her work is also global: she designed the 2018 MPavilion in Melbourne, the first public commission by a female architect in Australia.

La Massana Fine Arts School, Barcelona, Spain, 2017

LIESBETH VAN DER POL

Dok Architecten

Dutch architect van der Pol (b. 1959) was born in Amsterdam and graduated from the Delft University of Technology in 1988. She and Herman Zeinstra set up a practice in 1989, which merged in 2007 with Blue Architects Amsterdam to become Dok Architecten, whose projects include the Corten-steel-clad WKK power station in Utrecht (below). She was the first woman to be appointed chief government architect of the Netherlands, from 2008 to 2011. Van der Pol won the Charlotte Köhler Prize in 1992 and the Rotterdam-Maaskant Prize a year later.

WKK, Utrecht, The Netherlands, 2005

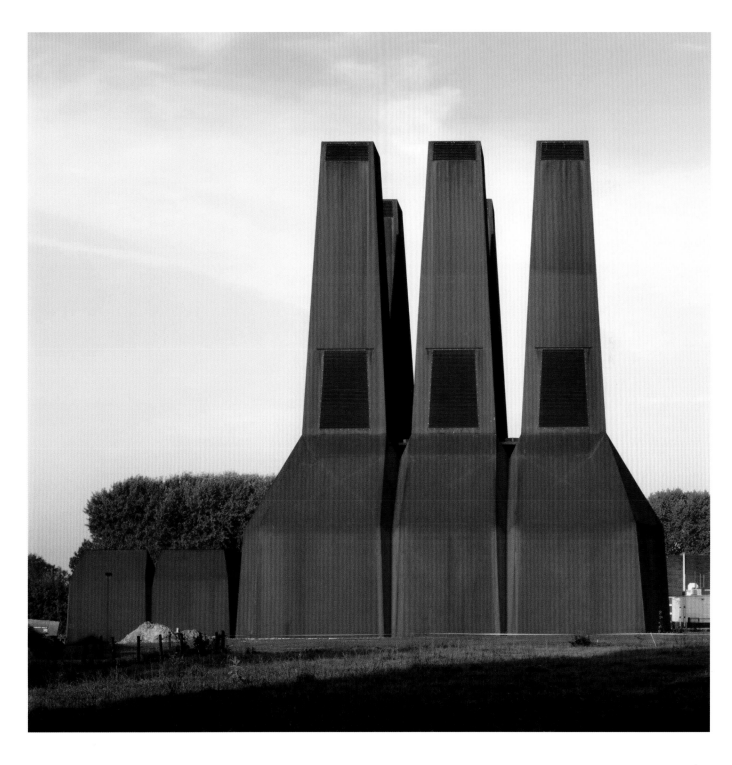

MÓNICA PONCE DE LEÓN

MPdL Studio

Ponce de León (b. 1965) is acknowledged as a leading light in the application of robotic technology in architectural education. She graduated from the University of Miami in 1989, with a master's degree from Harvard in 1991. She went on to teaching, at Harvard and the University of Houston among others. She established MPdL Studio in 2011, as well as becoming the dean at Princeton University School of Architecture in 2015. The futuristic-looking Helios House (below), an environmentally friendly gas station, won numerous prizes, including an American Institute of Architects Los Angeles Design Award.

Helios House, Los Angeles, California, USA, 2007

ELIZABETH DE PORTZAMPARC

De Portzamparc (n.d.) left Brazil, the country of her birth, in the late 1960s to live and study in France. She opened the Mostra gallery in Paris in 1986, integrating the fields of art, contemporary furniture design and architecture. She founded her own architectural agency the following year, and now has a broad selection of projects to her name, including street furniture for the Bordeaux tramway (2007), a new neighbourhood in Massy (2017) and the undulating Musée de la Romanité (below), all in France. A glass library for the Condorcet Campus in Aubervilliers, France, is due to be completed in 2020.

Musée de la Romanité, Nîmes, France, 2018

NO MATTER HOW MY WORK
WAS PUBLISHED OR CREDITED,
IT WAS SEEN AS VENTURI'S.
THE NOTION THAT WE MIGHT
BOTH DESIGN SEEMED
INCONCEIVABLE.

Denise Scott Brown

CECILIA PUGA

Puga (b. 1961) was born in Santiago, Chile, where she has run her own practice since 1995. Her work ranges in scale from offices for major companies to family homes, including the unusual Casa Bahía Azul (below), consisting of three volumes in the shape of a typical house, one inverted and resting on top of the other two. In 2009, she was among the 100 architects selected by Herzog & de Meuron to design a villa in Inner Mongolia, China, in the context of the Ordos 100 project, led by artist Ai Weiwei. In 2014, she won an international competition to restore the Pereira Palace in Santiago.

Casa Bahía Azul, Los Vilos, Chile, 2002

IVANKA RASPOPOVIĆ

Serbian Modernist architect Raspopović (1930–2015)
built her reputation on a series of large-scale public
and industrial projects in what was formerly Yugoslavia.
She graduated from the University of Belgrade
in 1954, and shortly after worked on the second phase
of the city's airport and an industrial complex in Priboj.
She collaborated with Ivan Antić to design Belgrade's
distinctive Museum of Contemporary Art (below) – a
building regarded as a national work of art, and for which
they were awarded an October Prize from the city.

Museum of Contemporary Art, Belgrade, Serbia, 1965,
with Ivan Antić

SONALI RASTOGI

Morphogenesis

Sonali Rastogi (b. 1967) founded Morphogenesis with Manit Rastogi in 1996, and grew the practice into one of India's largest and leading architectural firms. Morphogenesis has also been recognized internationally for its valuable contributions to contemporary architecture, winning a World Architecture Community Award in 2010 and the Singapore Institute of Architects Getz Architecture Prize in 2014. Rastogi herself is known as a prolific designer who has realized dozens of large-scale public buildings across the globe.

Pearl Academy of Fashion, Jaipur, India, 2009

LILLY REICH

German Modernist designer Reich (1885–1947) is best
known for being the professional and personal partner
of Ludwig Mies van der Rohe in the 1920s and 30s;
however, she was influential in her own right in the
Bauhaus movement and Deutscher Werkbund, and
had her own atelier. In collaboration with Mies, Reich
designed two of the twentieth century's most iconic
chairs, the Barcelona (1929) and Brno (1930). The pair
also designed the German National Pavilion for the
1929 Barcelona International Exhibition (below) – itself
now an emblematic work of the Modernist movement.

Barcelona Pavilion, Barcelona, Spain, 1929, with Ludwig
Mies van der Rohe

SU ROGERS

Su Rogers (b. 1939) was a key player in post-war architectural design and education. She has been partner in numerous practices including Team 4 (1963–7); Richard + Su Rogers Architects (1967–70); and Colquhoun, Miller & Partners, later John Miller + Partners (1986–2011). In collaboration with Richard Rogers and Renzo Piano, Su contributed to the competition-winning design of the Pompidou Centre (1977) in Paris. Residential projects Creek Vean (p. 69) and High-Tech holiday home Pillwood House (below) – both in Feock, southern Cornwall – are heritage-listed and considered important works of twentieth-century British architecture.

Pillwood House, Feock, England, UK, 1974, with John Miller

MARLIES ROHMER

Marlies Rohmer Architects & Urbanists

Rohmer (b. 1957) is a Dutch architect who founded her
practice, Marlies Rohmer Architects & Urbanists, in
Amsterdam in 1986. Her impressively diverse portfolio
ranges from large-scale inner-city developments to
schools, houses, a mosque, utility buildings (such as
a police station and a swimming pool), residential
care complexes and interior projects, as well as one
of the firm's most distinctive projects, a sports hall
(below) with an undulating facade. In 2008, Rohmer
was awarded the Amsterdam Prize for the Arts for
her contribution to art in the city.

Sports Block, Groningen, The Netherlands, 2014

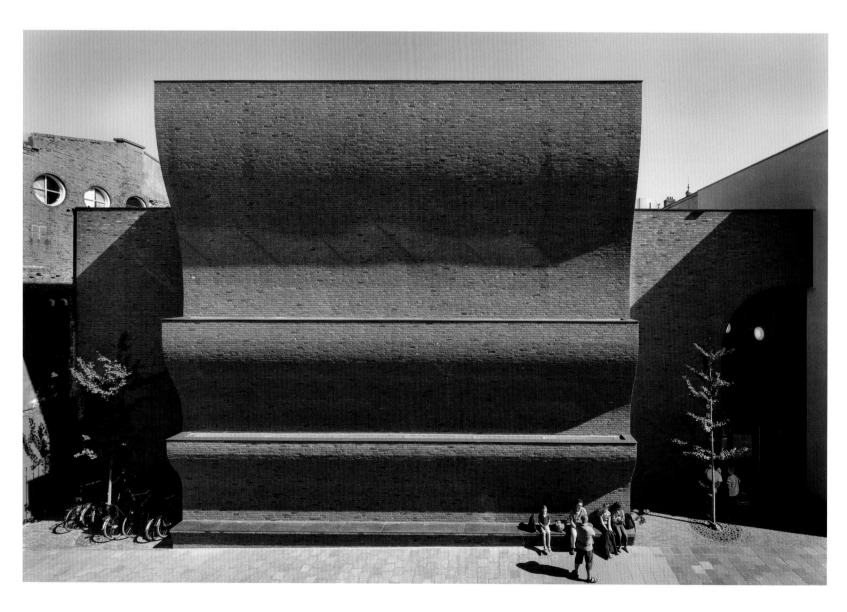

NATHALIE ROZENCWAJG

NAME Architecture

Rozencwajg (b. 1975) was born in Luxembourg and grew up in Brussels. She graduated from the Architectural Association School in London in 2001 and founded RARE Architects with Michel da Costa Gonçalves in 2005. Projects such as the Town Hall Hotel (below), which consists of a new wing wrapped entirely with a laser-cut, powder-coated aluminium skin, were awarded several prizes, including a 2011 Royal Institute of British Architects Award. In 2018, Rozencwajg founded a new firm, NAME Architecture.

Town Hall Hotel, London, England, UK, 2010

FLORA RUCHAT-RONCATI

FRR

Swiss architect Ruchat-Roncati (1937–2012) was a
pioneering figure in the Ticinese School of architecture,
working in the Ticino region of Switzerland, which
was influential in the mid-1970s, mixing a Modernist
zeal with sensitivity to the traditional. She graduated
in 1954 from the ETH (Institute of Technology) Zurich,
where she became the first woman professor and
chair of Architecture and Design in 1985. She set up
her own studio, FRR, designing the famous outdoor
baths at Bellinzona, Switzerland (1971), and various
tunnel structures along the Transjurane motorway
(below) through the Jura mountains.

Transjurane motorway, Jura, Switzerland, from 1988

NICOLA RUTT

Hawkins\Brown

British architect Rutt (b. 1972) studied at Kingston University and the University of Westminster, qualifying in 2001. She joined London-based practice Hawkins\ Brown a year earlier, becoming a partner in 2010. The firm puts emphasis on designing socially sustainable spaces. Rutt led the Here East project (below), which saw the press and broadcast facilities at the Olympic Park in east London transformed into a new community for digital innovators. The project has won several high-profile awards, including the AJ100 Building of the Year in 2018.

Here East, London, England, UK, 2018

HILARY SAMPLE

MOS Architects

Sample (b. 1971) graduated from Syracuse University in 1994, and founded New York-based MOS Architects – one of today's most influential young firms – with Michael Meredith in 2003. The duo's work is developed through playful experimentation and serious research, and spans from houses to cultural institutions and museum installations. Alongside their architectural work, MOS also creates books, furniture and software projects. The practice has received a number of important awards, including the 2015 National Design Award from the Cooper Hewitt, Smithsonian Design Museum.

Museum of Outdoor Arts Element House, Anton Chico, New Mexico, USA, 2014

MARGOT SCHÜRMANN

Joachim Schürmann Architekten

German architect Margot Schürmann (1924–98) was born in Ludwigshafen am Rhein and later studied in Munich and Darmstadt until 1949. In collaboration with Joachim Schürmann she went on to create some fine examples of Modernist architecture. Their projects included the brutalist Church of St Pius X (below) and the Post Office in Cologne (1992). Margot and Joachim were awarded the German Architecture Prize in 1981 and 1991, and the Grand BDA Prize, posthumously for Margot, in 2008.

Church of St Pius X, Neuss, Germany, 1967

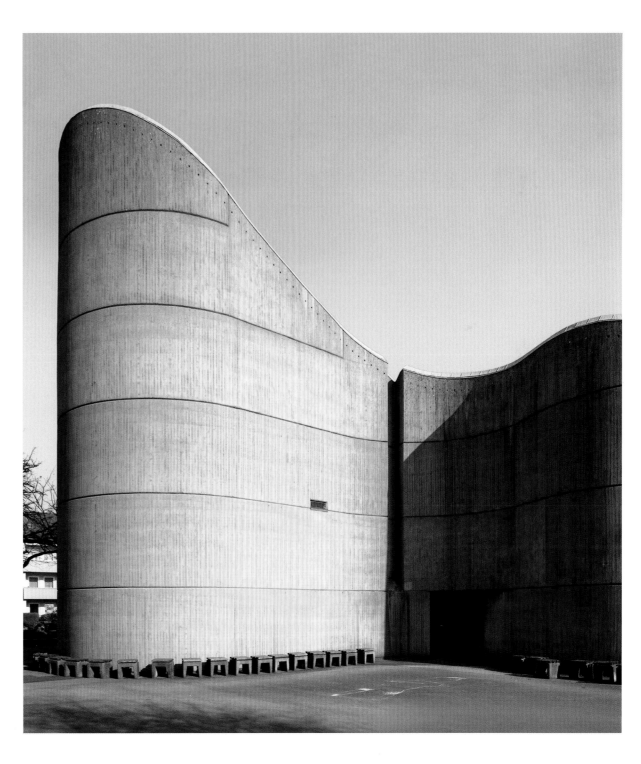

DENISE SCOTT BROWN

Venturi, Scott Brown & Associates

Scott Brown (b. 1931) graduated from the Architectural
Association School of Architecture in London in
1955. Since 1967, she has been a principal of the firm
Venturi, Scott Brown & Associates, alongside Robert
Venturi. The duo collaborated for half a century, and
many of their projects are now icons of postmodern
architecture. Scott Brown's and Venturi's influential and
controversial book, *Learning from Las Vegas* (1972), is
a seminal postmodern text.

↓   Franklin Court, Philadelphia, Pennsylvania, USA, 1976
→   Gordon Wu Hall, Princeton, New Jersey, USA, 1983
↘   Provincial Capitol Building, Toulouse, France, 1999

KAZUYO SEJIMA

SANAA

Sejima (b. 1956) is a Japanese architect who founded Kazuyo Sejima & Associates in 1987. In partnership with Ryue Nishizawa, she founded SANAA (Sejima and Nishizawa and Associates) in 1995. SANAA is renowned for works characterized by a minimalist aesthetic and structural delicacy. In 2010, Sejima was appointed curator of the Venice Architecture Biennale, the first woman ever to be offered the appointment. In the same year, she was awarded the Pritzker Prize – becoming only the second female recipient, after Zaha Hadid (p. 83), in the award's forty-year history.

↓   Sumida Hokusai Museum, Tokyo, Japan, 2017
→   New Museum, New York City, New York, USA, 2007
↓↓ Grace Farms, New Canaan, Connecticut, USA, 2015

WHEN I'M DESIGNING I NEVER THINK ABOUT BEING EITHER A WOMAN OR A MAN.

Cini Boeri

ANNABELLE SELLDORF

Selldorf Architects

German-born, New York-based Selldorf (b. 1960) founded Selldorf Architects in 1988. The firm came to international prominence with the opening of New York's Neue Galerie in 2001 and has since become known for creating galleries, cultural projects and private homes utilizing an elegant, Modernist aesthetic and subtle detailing. The practice also undertakes interior design, exhibition design, masterplanning and landscape concepts. Selldorf was the recipient of the 2016 Medal of Honor from the American Institute of Architects in 2017.

Pika House, Dunton Springs, Colorado, USA, 2004

BRIGITTE SHIM

Shim-Sutcliffe Architects

Canadian architect Shim (b. 1958) was born in Jamaica and met Howard Sutcliffe at the University of Waterloo in Ontario. The duo set up Shim-Sutcliffe Architects in Toronto in 1994, developing a design practice that reflects their shared interest in the integration and interrelated scales of architecture, landscape, and interior and industrial design. Their work includes projects for non-profit groups as well as private clients. Shim is a professor at the University of Toronto and, in 2012, received the Order of Canada for 'structures that enrich the public realm'.

Ravine Guest House, Toronto, Ontario, Canada, 2004

MINNETTE DE SILVA

De Silva (1918–98) was the first Sri Lankan woman
to train as an architect and, in 1948, became the first
Asian woman to be elected an associate of the Royal
Institute of British Architects. She was born in Ceylon
(now Sri Lanka), starting her career in India in 1938.
De Silva travelled widely, made influential contacts and
co-founded an arts magazine, *Marg*, in 1945. She set
up a practice in her home country in 1948, and gained
a reputation as a pioneer of the Modern style.

Senanayake Flats, Colombo, Sri Lanka, 1957

CHARLOTTE SKENE CATLING

Skene Catling de la Peña

Skene Catling (b. 1965) co-founded Skene Catling de la Peña, where she is an architect and director, with Jaime de la Peña in London in 2003. The practice is known for integrating contemporary projects into heritage-listed buildings, such as the Perm World Heritage Site in Russia (2010). The Flint House (below), a wedge-shaped residence clad in flint arranged in graduating tones, won the Royal Institute of British Architects House of the Year award in 2015. Skene Catling teaches at the Karlsruhe Institute of Technology in Germany.

Flint House, Waddesdon, England, UK, 2015

NORMA MERRICK SKLAREK

Sklarek (1926–2012) was the first African American woman to be licensed as an architect in New York (1954) and California (1962). She graduated from Columbia University in 1950, joining the New York Department of Public Works and then Skidmore, Owings and Merrill (SOM) from 1955. She moved to Los Angeles in 1960 to take up a role at Gruen and Associates, working closely with César Pelli on projects such as the Pacific Design Center (below) and the US Embassy in Tokyo (1976). In 1985, she founded Siegel Sklarek Diamond, the country's largest all-female architectural firm at the time.

Pacific Design Center, Los Angeles, California, USA, 1978, with César Pelli

ALISON SMITHSON

Alison and Peter Smithson

Alison Smithson (1928–93) was – along with Peter Smithson – half of one of the most formidable and influential architectural partnerships of the post-war period. Renowned for introducing 'New Brutalism' to Britain, the Smithsons were concerned with what they referred to as 'an ethic, not an aesthetic' in their architecture, which prioritized people and their experiences of a building over stylistic distractions. Their impact on the architectural scene in Britain, and abroad, was enormous.

← School at Hunstanton, Norfolk, England, UK, 1954
↙ Robin Hood Gardens, London, England, UK, 1972

BRINDA SOMAYA

Somaya & Kalappa Consultants

Indian architect Somaya (b. 1949) established the practice Somaya & Kalappa Consultants (SNK) in 1978 in a Mumbai garden shed, working with her sister Ranjini Kalappa until 1981. Somaya's work combines architecture, conservation and social responsibility. Clients include Tata Industries, for which Somaya designed a stadium that seats a thousand people (below), and the Louis Kahn complex in Ahmedabad, India, undertaking a restoration and conservation exercise. Somaya is a professor at Cornell University in the US.

↓ Olympic Swimming Pool and Stadium, Mumbai, India, 1986

MAYUMI WATANABE DE SOUZA LIMA

Souza Lima (1934–94) was born in Tokyo but moved to Brazil at the age of four, growing up in São Paulo, where she graduated from university in 1960. She gained a reputation for designing municipal buildings throughout the country, including the São Miguel Towers (below), in collaboration with iconic Brazilian architect Lelé. She also worked with Sérgio Souza Lima, including on some works for Lina Bo Bardi (p. 26). Souza Lima was a professor at the University of Brasília, among other institutions.

↓ São Miguel Towers, Brasilia, Brazil, 1994, with Lelé

ROSEMARY STJERNSTEDT

Stjernstedt (1912–98) was an English architect who is best known for her post-war housing in the UK, including the pioneering Alton East Estate in Roehampton (opposite) – considered Britain's most important social housing complex of the twentieth century – for which she led the design team. Stjernstedt graduated with a degree in architecture from the Birmingham School of Art in 1934, then moved to Sweden where she embarked on a career as a town planner. After the war, she returned to the UK to work for the London County Council, which at the time had a reputation as one of the most innovative city governments in the world.

→ Alton East Estate, London, England, UK, 1955

MARINA TABASSUM

Marina Tabassum Architects

Bangladesh-born Tabassum (b. 1968) is best known
for designing the Bait-ur-Rouf Mosque (below) –
built in brick using traditional methods – which won
the Aga Khan Award for Architecture in 2016, and
the Jameel Prize for contemporary Islamic design
in 2018. Tabassum graduated from the Bangladesh
University of Engineering and Technology in 1994, the
following year establishing a practice, Urbana, with
Kashef Chowdhury, and founded her eponymous firm
in 2005. She has been the academic director of the
Bengal Institute for Architecture, Landscapes and
Settlements since 2015.

Bait-ur-Rouf Mosque, Dhaka, Bangladesh, 2012

BENEDETTA TAGLIABUE

Miralles Tagliabue EMBT

Milan-born Tagliabue (b. 1963) co-founded Miralles Tagliabue EMBT in Barcelona with Enric Miralles, a studio that places special emphasis on the coherence between the built environment and public space. Following Miralles's death in 2000, Tagliabue took sole control of the company and has since worked on iconic projects across Europe and the Far East. She won the Royal Institute of British Architects Charles Jencks Award, for her major contribution to both the theory and practice of architecture, in 2013.

↓   Scottish Parliament Building, Edinburgh, Scotland, UK, 2001
↓↓ Santa Caterina Market, Barcelona, Spain, 2005

YUI TEZUKA

Tezuka Architects

Yui Tezuka (b. 1969) studied at the Musashi Institute of Technology in Yokohama and the Bartlett School of Architecture (University College London) before establishing Tokyo-based firm Tezuka Architects with Takaharu Tezuka in 1994. Their projects range from religious spaces to clinics and private houses, but the studio is especially well known for designing a number of inventive kindergartens and nursery schools. Fuji Kindergarten (below), with a roof deck that doubles as an outdoor space, was selected as the best school in the world by the United Nations' educational, scientific and cultural agency, UNESCO.

Fuji Kindergarten, Tachikawa, Tokyo, Japan, 2007

SUSANA TORRE

Argentinian-born Torre (b. 1944) is an academic and teacher who moved to New York in 1968 to pursue postgraduate studies at Columbia University. A revolutionary figure, Torre advocated the recognition of women in architecture – notably curating the 1977 exhibition *Women in American Architecture: A Historic and Contemporary Perspective* and editing a book of the same name. With Fire Station Five (below), she became the first female architect to design a building in the Modernist enclave of Columbus, Indiana.

Fire Station Five, Columbus, Indiana, USA, 1987

BILLIE TSIEN

Tod Williams Billie Tsien Architects

Tsien (b. 1949) co-founded her practice with Tod Williams in New York in 1986; the duo believe that 'architecture is the coming together of art and use.' The sculptural facade of the American Folk Art Museum (opposite), for example, was made of specially cast panels of white bronze. Their studio focuses on work for institutions including schools, museums and not-for-profit organizations. Tsien graduated in fine arts in 1971 from Yale. She is now president of the Architectural League of New York and has been director of the Public Art Fund in the US.

↓ The Barnes Foundation, Philadelphia, Pennsylvania, USA, 2012
→ American Folk Art Museum, New York City, New York, USA, 2001

I AM LOOKING FORWARD TO A TIME WHEN IT IS NOT NECESSARY TO CREATE SEPARATE AWARDS DEDICATED TO WOMEN ARCHITECTS.

Manuelle Gautrand

ELISA VALERO

Spanish architect Valero (b. 1971) graduated from the University of Valladolid in 1996. She opened her own office opposite the Alhambra in Granada in 1997. Her projects include the Dominican School in Ogíjares (2012), built within a restored heritage building; a minimal kindergarten in La Chana (2010); and a concrete church (below) – all in Granada. Valero was awarded the prestigious Swiss Architectural Award in 2018, and is a professor of architectural design at the Superior Technical School of Architecture in Granada.

Church in Playa Granada, Spain, 2016

SIIRI VALLNER

Kavakava

Vallner (b. 1972) is a founding member of Estonian practice Kavakava, which she leads alongside Indrek Peil. Many of the firm's major works are the result of public competitions. Notable projects include the Lasnamäe Track and Field Centre (below); Museum of Occupations (2003), one of her first built works; and the University of Tartu Narva College (2013), for which the studio was awarded the Estonian National Culture Award in 2013. Vallner received the Young Architect Award of the Estonian Architects Association in 2008.

Lasnamäe Track and Field Centre, Tallinn, Estonia, 2003

MARIE-JOSÉ VAN HEE

Marie-José Van Hee Architecten

Ghent-born Van Hee (b. 1950) is one of Belgium's most accomplished architects. Graduating from the Sint-Lucas Institute in 1974, she was associated with the so-called 'silencieux' group, concerned with the classical elements of composition and spatial geometry. Van Hee established her practice in 1975, working on public spaces, including MoMu (2002), Antwerp's fashion museum, as well as numerous subtly crafted residences, such as House DF (below). Since 1990, she has collaborated closely with Robbrecht & Daem Architecten, and they jointly received the Flemish Culture Prize in 1997.

House DF, Zuidzande, The Netherlands, 2007

ŠPELA VIDEČNIK

OFIS Architects

Videčnik (b. 1971) established OFIS Architects in 1996 with Rok Oman after studying at Ljubljana School of Architecture and London's Architectural Association. The practice often employs a strategy of using restrictions as a starting point for creativity and innovation – hence its frequent participation in design competitions, resulting in projects such as 185 student housing units in Paris (2008) and the amorphous Borisov Football Stadium Arena (below). Videčnik teaches at the Harvard Graduate School of Design in the US.

Football Stadium Arena, Borisov, Belarus, 2014

PAOLA VIGANÒ

Studio Associato Bernardo Secchi Paola Viganò

Viganò (b. 1961) is an Italian architect who became the first woman to win France's Grand Prix de l'Urbanisme, in 2013. She graduated in 1987, then studied at the University of Venice (IUAV) for her PhD. She founded her practice with Bernardo Secchi in 1990, and their urban-planning projects have changed the faces of Bergamo, Siena, Antwerp, Saint-Nazaire and other cities. Viganò is a professor of Urbanism at IUAV and of Urban Theory and Urban Design at the EPFL (Swiss Federal Institute of Technology) Lausanne.

↓   Theaterplein, Antwerp, Belgium, 2008

NATHALIE DE VRIES

MVRDV

Dutch architect and urbanist de Vries (b. 1965) has a global status, having co-founded the progressive studio MVRDV in Rotterdam in 1993 with Winy Maas and Jacob van Rijs. The practice has designed a wide range of building types: from private residences to skyscrapers, cultural institutions and public projects, including the Silodam (opposite, top), a mixed-use building, and the cantilevered Balancing Barn (opposite, bottom), clad in reflective steel tiles. De Vries is the president of the Royal Institute of Dutch Architects and has taught widely, including at the Kunstakademie Düsseldorf and Harvard in the US.

→   Silodam, Amsterdam, The Netherlands, 2003
↘   Balancing Barn, Thorington, England, UK, 2010

MARION WEISS

Weiss/Manfredi

Weiss (b. 1957) studied at Yale and the University of Virginia, and, with Michael Manfredi, entered a competition in 1989 to design a memorial to military women at Arlington National Cemetery in Virginia, USA. The duo won, and set up Weiss/Manfredi in New York. The firm now has an international portfolio of large-scale projects recognized for their spatial and material invention. Their architectural drawings for the acclaimed Olympic Sculpture Park in Seattle (2001) are held by the Museum of Modern Art (MoMA). Weiss is also a professor at the University of Pennsylvania.

← Tata Innovation Center at Cornell Tech, New York City, New York, USA, 2017

SARAH WIGGLESWORTH

Sarah Wigglesworth Architects

Wigglesworth (b. 1957) is widely acknowledged as a pioneering influence in British architecture and is particularly known for her extensive experience in sustainable design. Her approach is epitomized in projects such as the Stock Orchard Street house in London (2001) and the Bermondsey Bicycle Store (below), aiming to embed green transport values within the local community. Until 2016, Wigglesworth was professor of architecture at the University of Sheffield, where she led research into the design of exemplary neighbourhoods for older people.

↓ Bermondsey Bicycle Store, London, England, UK, 2008

ELIZABETH WRIGHT INGRAHAM

Elizabeth Wright Ingraham & Associates

Wright Ingraham (1922–2013), the granddaughter of
Frank Lloyd Wright, met Gordon Ingraham at Taliesin
and the pair worked together in Colorado Springs
throughout the 1950s and 60s. She was influenced by
Ludwig Mies van der Rohe, with whom she studied at
the Armour Institute in Chicago (now the Illinois Institute
of Technology). She formed her own firm in 1983, and
her notable later projects include La Casa residence
(below). Wright Ingraham was also recognized as an
influential educator and community activist.

La Casa, Pueblo West, Colorado, USA, 1995

ADA YVARS BRAVO

Mangera Yvars Architects

Yvars Bravo (n.d.) graduated from the Barcelona School of Architecture and subsequently worked at David Chipperfield Architects, before co-founding Mangera Yvars Architects, which has offices in Barcelona and London, with Ali Mangera in 2011. Her projects range from a university in Qatar and a housing complex in Madagascar to hilltop residences in Barcelona (all 2013) and the Qatar Faculty of Islamic Studies (below), described as a beacon of knowledge and prayer.

Qatar Faculty of Islamic Studies, Doha, Qatar, 2013

I THINK IT'S A GREAT RELEASE TO REALIZE THAT ARCHITECTURE IS MUCH BIGGER THAN THE INDIVIDUAL, THAT IT'S AN ENORMOUS TRADITION THAT YOU ARE JUST A VERY TINY PART OF.

Shelley McNamara

CAZÚ ZEGERS

Cazú Zegers Arquitectura

Chilean architect Zegers (b. 1958) graduated from the Catholic University of Valparaíso in 1984, moving to New York to study at the Parsons School of Design. She returned to Chile in 1990 to set up her own studio in Santiago, where her approach is inspired by the relationship between architecture and poetry, and influenced by her Chilean upbringing. The circular, concrete Casa Do (below) exudes calm and is built with a remarkable level of precision. Zegers also uses reclaimed wood in many projects, such as Casa Esmeralda (2014), a timber box-on-stilts, and Casa LLU (2018), an isolated retreat.

Casa Do, Los Vilos, Chile, 2000

DI ZHANG

WAA (We Architech Anonymous)

Di Zhang (n.d.) studied at the Bartlett School of
Architecture (University College London) and
the University of Sheffield – both in the UK. In 2010,
she co-founded the architecture practice WAA in
Beijing with Jack Young. The duo's work aims to be
flexible and unimposing. The ribbon-like facade
of MOCA (below), for example, draws on the site's
geology and layers of sediment left by the receding
river. Di Zhang was shortlisted for the Moira Gemmill
Prize for Emerging Architecture from the Women
in Architecture awards in 2016.

Yinchuan Museum of Contemporary Art (MOCA),
Yinchuan City, Ningxia, China, 2015

TIMELINE

1912

Marion Mahony Griffin, p. 126

1918

Margaret Kropholler, p. 110

1925

Jakoba Mulder, p. 140

1929

Barbara Brukalska, p. 38

Eileen Gray, p. 82

1938

Lilly Reich, p. 160

Margaret Justin Blanco White, p. 22

1947

Julia Morgan, p. 136

1949

Ray Eames, p. 57

1951

Lina Bo Bardi, p. 26

1954

Mary Medd, p.131

Alison Smithson, p.180

1955

Rosemary Stjernstedt, p.183

1957

Minnette de Silva, p.177

1960

Natalie de Blois, p.24

1963

Altuğ Çinici, p.45

1964

Jane Drew, p.56

Judith Edelman, p.58

1965

Ivanka Raspopović, p.158

1966

Wendy Foster, p.69

1967

Cini Boeri, p.30

Elisabeth Böhm, p.31

Margot Schürmann, p.167

1968

Lina Bo Bardi, pp.28–9

Zofia Hansen, p.86

Charlotte Perriand, p.148

1969

Inger Augusta Exner, p.63

1972

Kate Macintosh, p.125

Alison Smithson, p.180

1973

Grabowska-Hawrylak, p.80

1974

Su Rogers, p.161

1976

Patty Hopkins, p.95

Denise Scott Brown, p.168

1978

Norma Merrick Sklarek, p.179

1982

Maya Lin, p.116

1983

Denise Scott Brown, p.169

1985

Raili Pietilä, p.149

1986

Lina Bo Bardi, p.27

Eva Koppel, p.109

Brinda Somaya, p.181

1987

Susana Torre, p.189

1988

Flora Ruchat-Roncati, p.164

1991

Patricia Patkau, p.147

1993

Kathryn Findlay, p.68

1994

Itsuko Hasegawa, p.88

1995

Mayumi Watanabe de Souza Lima, p.182

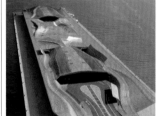

Brit Andresen, p.14

Farshid Moussavi, p.138

Elizabeth Wright Ingraham, p.202

1996

Margarethe Heubacher-Sentobe, p.91

1997

Anne Lacaton, p.112

MJ Long, p.121

1999

Louisa Hutton, p.101

Denise Scott Brown, p.169

2000

Julia Barfield, p.18

Anupama Kundoo, p.111

2001

Cazú Zegers, p.205

Regine Leibinger, p.115

Benedetta Tagliabue, p.185

Billie Tsien, p.191

2002

Lise Anne Couture, p.46

2003

Elizabeth Diller, p. 54

Paola Maranta, p. 130

Cecilia Puga, p. 157

Siiri Vallner, p. 194

Nathalie de Vries, p. 199

2004

Sharon Johnston, p. 104

Annabelle Selldorf, p. 175

Brigitte Shim, p. 176

2005

Zaha Hadid, p. 83

Ellen van Loon, p. 122

2006

Liesbeth van der Pol, p. 153

Benedetta Tagliabue, pp. 186–7

Deborah Berke, p. 20

Anna Heringer, p. 90

Annabel Lahz, p. 113

2007

Sara de Giles, p. 77

Toshiko Mori, p. 137

Mónica Ponce de León, p. 154

Kazuyo Sejima, p. 171

Yui Tezuka, p. 188

2008

Marie-José Van Hee, p. 195

Yvonne Farrell and Shelley McNamara, p. 64

Lu Wenyu, p. 123

Débora Mesa, p. 132

Sheila O'Donnell, p. 144

Paola Viganó, p. 198

2009

Sarah Wigglesworth, p. 201

Sharon Johnston, p. 104

Momoyo Kaijima, p. 106

Doriana Mandrelli Fuksas, p. 127

Sonali Rastogi, p. 159

2010

Frida Escobedo, p. 61

Débora Mesa, p. 133

Belén Moneo, pp. 134–5

Nathalie Rozencwajg, p. 163

2011

Nathalie de Vries, p. 199

Eliana Beltrán, Catalina Patiño and Viviana Peña, p. 19

Teresa Borsuk, p. 33

Lucía Cano, p. 41

Dang Qun, p. 48

Silvia Gmür, p. 79

Maria Giuseppina Grasso Cannizzo, p. 81

Francine Houben, p. 97

Eva Jiřičná, p. 103

Fuensanta Nieto, p. 143

2012

Tatiana Bilbao, p. 21

Sook Hee Chun, p. 44

Dang Qun, p. 49

Odile Decq, p. 51

Julie Eizenberg, p. 59

Saija Hollmén, Jenni Reuter and Helena Sandman, p. 93

Carla Juaçaba, p.105

Ilse Maria Königs, p.108

Jing Liu, p.118

Farshid Moussavi, p.139

Yuko Nagayama, p.141

Marina Tabassum, p.184

2013

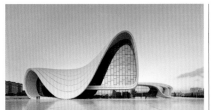

Billie Tsien, p.190

Louise Braverman, pp.34–5

Olga Felip, p.67

Ángela García de Paredes, p.72

Zaha Hadid, pp.84–5

Francine Houben, p.97

Patricia Patkau, p.146

Ada Yvars Bravo, p.203

2014

Alice Casey, p.43

Angela Deuber, p.53

Petra Gipp, p.78

Naoko Horibe, p.96

Marlies Rohmer, p.162

Hilary Sample, p.166

2015

Špela Videčnik, pp.196–7

Gloria Cabral, p.39

Gabriela Carrillo, p.42

Sharon Davis, p.50

Odile Decq, p. 51

Elizabeth Diller, p. 55

Farrell and
McNamara, p. 65

Manuelle Gautrand, p. 73

Beate Hølmebakk, p. 94

Eleena Jamil, p. 102

Sheila O'Donnell, p. 145

Kazuyo Sejima, pp. 172–3

Charlotte Skene Catling, p. 178

2016

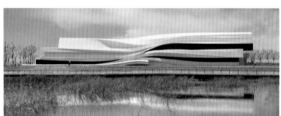

Di Zhang, pp. 206–7

Sandra Barclay, p. 15

Sandra Barclay, p. 16–7

Tatiana Bilbao, p. 21

Camilla Block, p. 23

Alison Brooks, pp. 36–7

Sumaya Dabbagh, p. 47

Gabriela Etchegaray,
p. 62

Jeanne Gang, p. 70

Jeanne Gang, p. 71

Lina Ghotmeh, pp. 74–5

Mojgan and
Gisue Hariri, p. 87

Mimi Hoang, p. 92

Rossana Hu, p. 99

Anouk Legendre, p. 114

Nerma Linsberger, p. 117

Jing Liu, p. 118

Inês Lobo, p. 119

2017

Carme Pigem, p. 150

Elisa Valero, p. 193

Shirley Blumberg, p. 25

Fernanda Canales, p. 40

Sofía von Ellrichshausen, p. 60

Stephanie Macdonald, p. 124

Dorte Mandrup, pp. 128–9

Carme Pigem, p. 151

Carme Pinós, p. 152

2018

Kazuyo Sejima, p. 170

Marion Weiss, p. 200

Amale Andraos, p. 13

Frida Escobedo, p. 61

Róisín Heneghan, p. 89

Huang Wenjing, p. 100

2019

Mariam Kamara, p. 107

Elizabeth de Portzamparc, p. 155

Nicola Rutt, p. 165

Stephanie Macdonald, p. 124

QUOTATIONS

Numerals refer to page numbers

6 In 2003, the MAK (Museum for Applied Arts) in Vienna presented an exhibition titled *Zaha Hadid. Architecture,* documenting how the architect conquered design resources that were beyond the supposed remit of the discipline proper. Attendants wore t-shirts emblazoned with quotes by Hadid (p. 83), including 'Would they still call me a diva if I was a man?'

12 Dorte Mandrup (p. 128) argues that the prefix 'woman' detracts from the occupation of being an architect. In an opinion piece published on *Dezeen* on 27 May 2017, Mandrup contends that the term implies a lack of competition, or ability, as a consequence of gender.

32 From an interview with Christina Pazzanese published in the *Harvard Gazette* on 16 May 2018, in which Toshiko Mori (p. 137) discusses her early life in Japan and how her interest in art led to her first experiences with architecture.

52 From an article by Edwin Heathcote titled 'Zaha Hadid Blazes Trail for Women with RIBA Architecture Award' published in the *Financial Times* on 24 September 2015. Hadid (p. 83) speaks about her difficulty being accepted as part of the establishment on the event of being awarded the Royal Institute of British Architects Royal Gold Medal for architecture.

66 From a transcribed roundtable discussion at which eight architects – including Norma Merrick Sklarek (p. 179) – from nationally recognized firms around the US discussed issues facing women in architecture at the time. The conversation formed part of an article titled 'Women in Corporate Firms' written by Nancy Solomon and published in *Architecture* magazine in October 1991.

76 From an interview with Oliver Wainwright published in the *Guardian* on 20 October 2017, in which Elizabeth Diller (p. 54) speaks about Diller Scofidio + Renfro's selection as the designers of the new £250m Centre for Music in London, UK. The piece is titled 'Meet Liz Diller, the Rebel Architect Behind MoMA, the High Line and Now a Home for Simon Rattle.'

98 From an article published in the *Financial Times* on 13 July 2018 to celebrate Itsuko Hasegawa (p. 88) winning the Royal Academy's inaugural Architecture Prize for lifetime achievement.

120 From an article titled 'Snubbed, Cheated, Erased: The Scandal of Architecture's Invisible Women' by Oliver Wainwright published in the *Guardian* on 16 October 2018. The story presented a number of examples of women who have been written out of history, including the Dutch artist Madelon Vriesendorp (pp. 8–9). Vriesendorp was a co-founder of Office of Metropolitan Architecture (OMA) in the early 1970s. One of her most memorable works for the practice – *Flagrant Délit*, a drawing depicting two skyscrapers post copulation – is often credited to Rem Koolhaas, her partner at OMA.

142 Speaking about the state of the architecture industry in the UK, Farshid Moussavi (p. 138) rejects the need for female role models. From a think piece titled 'Farshid Moussavi on Women in Architecture' published in the *Architectural Review* on 28 May 2012.

156 From an interview with Stephanie Salomon and Steve Kroeter published in *Designers & Books* on 7 January 2014. Denise Scott Brown (p. 168) describes the making of her seminal work *Learning from Las Vegas* (Cambridge: MIT Press, 1972), which she wrote with her partner Robert Venturi along with architect Steven Izenour. Venturi won the Pritzker Prize in 1991, however Scott Brown was overlooked for the award. A campaign by students at Harvard has recently attempted and failed to have Scott Brown retroactively credited.

174 In this interview titled 'Designing is a Joy but also a Commitment' with Margherita Guccione for *Domus* published on 9 May 2012, Cini Boeri (p. 30) touches on themes including architecture as a moral ethic and joy as a design aesthetic.

192 Manuelle Gautrand (p. 73) reflects on winning Women Architect of the Year, awarded by Arvha, in 2014 in an interview with *Aesthetica* magazine published on 24 June 2015.

204 Shelley McNamara (p. 64) of Grafton Architects covers a range of topics in this interview with *Design Boom*, published on 27 February 2013, including her early interest in architecture and the importance of public space.

FURTHER READING

Where are all the Women Architects? is a common by-line in articles and books which seek to question the absence of gender parity in the industry. As the number of women architects continues to fall, one answer can be found in the work of those who play a significant role in practice through discourse and writing, particularly in relation to gender, rather than through building. In addition to a reading list, this section brings together a number of biographies of those who have been influential in shaping the built environment in alternative ways, highlighting how women have historically challenged the terms in which women's work in architecture operates within an otherwise distinctly male discourse.

The list however reflects the dominance of English speaking language and Western criticism in the profession, and the effectiveness of American and European pedagogies in defining architectural practice worldwide. As such, like the buildings featured in the main body of the book, it is intended to act as a starting point to encourage those who have picked up this volume to actively seek more information and find others who continue to shape the profession elsewhere, both within and outside its conventions.

Agrawal, Pooja. Public Practice
publicpractice.org.uk

Agrawal is co-founder of Public Practice, a not-for-profit social enterprise with a mission to improve the quality and equality of everyday places by building the public sector's capacity for proactive planning. Among her many roles, Agrawal is a trustee of the Museum of Architecture and a member of the Design South East Panel, both based in London, UK. She is also an advocate for diversity in the built environment sector.

Agrest, Diana et al. *The Sex of Architecture* (New York: Harry N Abrams, 1996)

New York-based Agrest is an architect and professor of architecture at the Irwin S Chanin School of Architecture at the Cooper Union. *The Sex of Architecture* is a compilation of texts that bring together the views of women in architecture and urbanism. Agrest's own research interests concern nature and urbanism.

Ainley, Rosa et al. *THIS IS WHAT WE DO: A Muf Manual* (London: Batsford, 2001)

This book outlines the working practices and projects of Muf. Founded by Liza Fior and Katherine Clarke in 1994, the practice specializes in public realm architecture and art, with an ambition to realize the potential pleasures that exist at the intersection between the lived and the built.

Al-Sabouni, Marwa. *The Battle for Home: The Vision of a Young Architect in Syria* (London: Thames & Hudson, 2016)

Al-Sabouni is an architect based in Syria. Her book *The Battle for Home* is a compelling explanation of the personal impact of conflict in the country, and offers hope for how architecture can play a role in rebuilding a sense of identity within a damaged society.

Baden-Powell, Charlotte. *The Architect's Pocket Book* (New York: Architectural Press, 1997)

Baden-Powell was trained at the Architectural Association in London, UK. She practised architecture for more than forty years. Her text *The Architect's Pocket Book* is a guide to building regulations, planning, measurement and detailing, and has sold more than 40,000 copies since it was first published in 1997.

___

Benedict Brown, James et al. *A Gendered Profession* (London: RIBA Publishing, 2017)

This book is an attempt to move the debate about gender in architecture beyond the tradition of gender-segregated diagnostic or critical discourse towards something more propositional, actionable and transformative. It does this by bringing together a comprehensive selection of essays from experts in architectural education and practice, touching on issues such as LGBT, family status and gender-biased awards.

___

Brown, Lori. *Feminist Practices: Interdisciplinary Approaches to Women in Architecture* (Farnham: Ashgate Publishing, 2011)

Brown's work investigates architecture's impact on everyday lives and the spaces in which architecture may not be immediately legible, such as within social and political institutions. For example, her book *Contested Space: Abortion Clinics, Women's Shelters and Hospitals* (London: Routledge, 2013) investigates how legislation affects politicized and securitized spaces. Brown is the founder of ArciteXX, a woman and architecture group based in New York, USA.

___

Burns, Karen. Parlour
archiparlour.org

Burns is a senior lecturer in architectural design at the University of Melbourne, Australia. She was instrumental in establishing Parlour: Women, Equity, Architecture, an organization promoting the visibility of women in the field. Burns has written profusely on feminist practices in architecture.

___

Colomina, Beatriz et al. *Sexuality and Space* (New York: Princeton Architectural Press, 1992)

Colomina is an architectural historian, theorist and curator. A professor at Princeton University, Colomina has written extensively on questions of architecture, art, technology, sexuality and media. She is a member of the collaborative research group Radical Pedagogies, which explores educational experiments that played a crucial role in shaping architectural discourse and practice in the second half of the twentieth century.

___

Cuff, Dana. *Architecture: The Story of Practice* (Cambridge: MIT Press, 1992)

Cuff is a professor and author, as well as practitioner of architecture. Her work focuses on affordable housing, suburban studies, the politics of place and the spatial implications of computer technologies. Cuff is also the founder of Citylab, a think tank that engages experimental design and research about the emerging metropolis.

___

Deamer, Peggy. *The Architect as Worker: Immaterial Labour, the Creative Class, and the Politics of Design* (London: Bloomsbury Academic, 2015)

Deamer is an architect and professor of Architecture at Yale University. She is a founding member of the Architecture Lobby, a group advocating for the value of architectural design and labour. Her book *The Architect as Worker* confronts the nature of architectural and design work, and addresses the invisibility of creative labour.

___

Desāī, Mādhavī. *Women Architects and Modernism in India: Narratives and Contemporary Practices* (Abingdon: Taylor & Francis, 2016)

Historically, studies on architecture in South Asia have ignored women in canonical histories of the discipline and continue to do so. This book recovers the stories of women architects whose careers nearly parallel the development of Modernism in colonial and postcolonial India. It is one of only a few volumes that detail women architects in the subcontinent, bringing together a number of case studies that highlight the work of those such as Perin Jamshedji Mistri (1913–89), Hema Sankalia (1934–2015) and Anupama Kundoo (p. 111), among others.

___

Easterling, Keller. *Extrastatecraft: The Power of Infrastructure Space* (London: Verso, 2014)

Easterling is an architect and writer, and professor at Yale University in New Haven, USA. Her book *Extrastatecraft* analyzes the politics of infrastructure and the invisible rules that govern the spaces of everyday life, revealing the strategies of an increasingly unaccountable modern world.

___

Frichot, Hélène. *Architecture and Feminisms: Ecologies, Economies, Technologies (Critiques: Critical Studies in Architectural Humanities)* (London: Routledge, 2017)

Frichot is professor in critical studies in architecture at the KTH Royal Institute of Technology in Stockholm. Her research examines the transdisciplinary field between architecture and philosophy with an emphasis on feminist theories and practices.

___

Friedman, Alice T. *Women and the Making of the Modern House: A Social and Architectural History* (New Haven: Yale University Press, 2006)

Friedman's work focuses on the history of European and North American architecture, with an emphasis on social history, gender and cultural studies. Her book *Women and the Making of the Modern House* investigates how women patrons of architecture were essential catalysts for innovation in domestic architectural design.

___

Greenwood, Jane. NYC LGBT Historic Sites Project
nyclgbtsites.org

As an advocate, Greenwood continues to speak on behalf of equality in the workplace, not only for women but also for ethnic minorities and the LGBTQ community. Having co-founded OLGAD (Organization of Lesbian + Gay Architects and Designers) in the 1990s, Greenwood is recognized as a pioneer in the struggle for visibility in the architecture profession for underrepresented individuals and their contributions, most notably leading to the formation of the NYC LGBT Historic Sites Project.

___

Heynen, Hilde et al. *Negotiating Domesticity: Spatial Productions of Gender in Modern Architecture* (London: Routledge, 2005)

Heynen is a professor of architectural theory at the KU Leuven in Belgium. Writing on the history and theory of modernity and Modernism, Heynen pays close attention to the intersection of architecture and gender. She is currently working on an intellectual biography of Sibyl Moholy-Nagy.

___

Huxtable, Ada Louise. *On Architecture: Collected Reflections on a Century of Change* (London: Walker Books, 2008)

Huxtable (1921-2013) was an architecture critic for the *New York Times* and the first woman named to the jury of experts for the Pritzker Prize between 1987 and 2005. She began her career at the Museum of Modern Art (MoMA) in New York, USA, under Philip Johnson who she admired but found shallow. Writing prolifically, Huxtable sought to bring architecture into the public sphere, informed not just by architecture but also real estate, commercial interests and politics.

___

Jacobs, Jane. *The Death and Life of Great American Cities* (New York: Random House, 1961)

New York-based Jacobs was an activist and writer whose work in the 1960s focused on the neighbourhood around her Greenwich Village home. Organizing grassroots eff-orts to prevent against slum clearance, Jacobs was instrumental in preventing the construction of the Lower Manhattan Expressway. She was arrested for her activism against the project in 1968.

___

De Klerk, Khensani. Matri-Archi(tecture)
matri-archi.com

De Klerk is an architect based in Cape Town, South Africa and founder of online platform Matri-Archi(tecture). Matri-Archi is an intersectional collective that brings African women of colour together for the empowerment of African cities through education. De Klerk states that her work is focused on developing tools for multiple identity groups to be active designers of space.

Lambert, Phyllis. Canadian Centre for Architecture
cca.qc.ca

Lambert is a Canadian architect and philanthropist responsible for recruiting Ludwig Mies van der Rohe to design the Seagram Tower in 1954 in New York, USA. Over the course of her career Lambert has invested in a number of heritage projects, founding in 1989 the Canadian Centre for Architecture (CCA) within which she is still active today. The CCA has become an important resource for architects worldwide due to its archives, publications and extensive public programme.

Lokko, Lesley, ed. *White Papers, Black Marks: Architecture, Race, Culture* (Minneapolis: University of Minnesota Press, 2000)

Lokko is an architect, academic and author of a number of novels. Head of school at the Graduate School of Architecture at the University of Johannesburg, South Africa, Lokko has been an ongoing contributor to discourses around identity, race and African urbanism. Her book *White Papers, Black Marks* charts the relationship between race and architecture, exploring how the notion of difference is crucial to understanding how the built environment is shaped.

MATRIX Feminist Design Cooperative. *Making Space: Women and the Man Made Environment* (London: Pluto Press, 1987)

Set up in the 1980s, MATRIX began as an architectural practice that grew out of the Feminist Design Collective in London, UK. MATRIX were one of the first groups to take a feminist stance on the built environment and gendered roles within its production. Members included Jos Boys, Frances Bradshaw, Jane Darke, Benedicte Foo, Sue Francis, Barbara McFarlane and Marion Roberts who ran the group as a workers' cooperative. Their intention was to work together as women on practical projects, completing the Jagonari Educational Resource Centre (1987) in London, UK.

McLeod, Mary. *Charlotte Perriand: An Art of Living* (New York: Abrams, 2003)

McLeod is a professor of architecture at Columbia University in New York, USA, where she teaches architecture history and theory. Her research and publications have focused on the history of the Modern movement and on contemporary architecture theory, examining issues concerning the connections between architecture and ideology.

Moholy-Nagy, Sibyl. *Matrix of Man: An Illustrated History of Urban Environment* (Santa Barbara: Praeger, 1968)

Moholy-Nagy (1903–71) was an art and architecture historian who was influential in reshaping Modernism in the postwar period. Her numerous articles and books focused on vernacular architecture and urban issues, providing a critical counterpoint to postwar Modernist architecture which she promoted through her posts at significant US universities, including the Pratt Institute and Columbia University, both in New York, USA.

MYCKET
mycket.org

Based in Sweden, MYCKET is an art and architecture collective founded by designers, architects and artists Mariana Alves Silva, Katarina Bonnevier and Thérèse Kristiansson. Their practice is focused on intersectional perspectives in art research, such as anti-racist and queer-feminist theory, uniquely informed by the theatrical, the carnivalesque and political activism.

PartW
part-w.com

Action group PartW campaigns for alternative nominees for the Royal Institute of British Architects Royal Gold Medal both past and present. It comprises a number of leading figures in the UK who have each spoken out against the gender disparity of the architecture profession.

Petrescu, Doina. *Altering Practices: Feminist Politics and Poetics of Space* (London: Routledge, 2007)

Petrescu's research focuses on, among other topics, co-design, civic participation, gendered practices and urban resilience. Her book *Altering Practices* addresses the emergence of social and political theories that raise questions of identity and difference, revisiting feminist concerns with space.

Pidgeon, Monica. Pidgeon Audiovisual Collection
pidgeondigital.com

Pidgeon (1939-2009) was a British interior designer and architectural writer best known for her role as editor of *Architectural Design* from 1946 to 1975. She was influential in publicizing the work of young architects in the UK in the early postwar period, including that of Alison and Peter Smithson (p. 181). In 1979 she set up the Pidgeon Audiovisual Collection, a series of recordings featuring architects and designers discussing their work, intended to be presented at architectural schools.

Rendell, Jane et al. *Reader: Gender, Space, Architecture* (London: Routledge, 1999)

Rendell's research at the Bartlett School of Architecture (University College London) concerns how writing and pedagogic practices intersect with art, architecture, feminism, history and psychoanalysis. Throughout her career she has been involved in feminist activism, including as a member of the group Taking Place.

Stead, Naomi. *Women, Practice, Architecture* (London: Routledge, 2014)

Stead is professor of architecture at Monash University in Melbourne. A widely published art and architectural critic in Australia, her research focus is on experimental writing practices and gender equity in architecture. Her book *Women, Practice, Architecture* argues that the image of the architect is gendered, exploring the working lives of women in the field and the terms in which popular media constructs the identity of the woman architect.

Stratigakos, Despina. *Where Are the Women Architects?* (New Jersey: Princeton University Press, 2016)

Stratigakos is a historian who has authored a number of books on the intersection of power and architecture. Much of her work concentrates on the challenges that women face in the profession. She is an advisor to the International Archive of Women in Architecture at Virginia Tech and a trustee of the Beverly Willis Architecture Foundation, both based in the US. Her book *Where Are the Women Architects?* explores the roles of women in the profession as well as detailing how a new generation is fighting against the tendency that excludes women from practice.

Sutton, Sharon. *When Ivory Towers Were Black: A Story about Race in America's Cities and Universities* (New York: Fordham University Press, 2017)

Sutton became an architecture educator in 1975, having taught at various institutions including the University of Michigan, USA, where she became the first African American woman to become a full professor in an accredited architectural degree programme. She is an advocate for participatory planning and design processes in disenfranchised communities and only the twentieth African American woman to be licensed to practice architecture in the US.

Taking Place
takingplace.org.uk

Defining itself as a feminist spatial practice, Taking Place comprises a group of women artists and architects who began working together in 2000 out of a shared interest in questions of gender and spatial practice. The group is connected through some of its members to MATRIX Feminist Design Cooperative. Members are Jos Boys, Julia Dwyer, Miche Fabre Lewin, Teresa Hoskyns, Katie Lloyd Thomas, Brigid McLeer, Angie Pascoe, Doina Petrescu, Jane Rendell, Sue Ridge and Helen Stratford.

Tyrwhitt, Jacqueline, ed. *Patrick Geddes in India* (London: Lund Humphries, 1947)

A town planner, journalist and educator, Tyrwhitt (1905–83) was an influential part of a transnational network of practitioners who established the postwar Modern movement. Tyrwhitt stated that Sir Patrick Geddes was perhaps the most important formative influence on her career. Geddes's use of 'thinking machines' and other diagrams made a particular impression on her, and she was instrumental in bringing Geddes's town planning theories to a wider audience after his death in 1932.

Walker, Lynne. *AA Women in Architecture: 1917–2017* (London: AA Publications, 2017)

This book marks the centenary of the admission of the first female students to the Architectural Association in London, UK. Walker is currently writing a history of gender, space and architecture in Britain from the seventeenth century to the present.

Wigglesworth, Sarah et al. *Desiring Practices: Architecture, Gender and the Interdisciplinary* (London: Black Dog Publishing, 1996)

This book aims to introduce a gendered awareness of architectural practice through criticism, architecture and psychoanalysis, and politics. Its editors include Wigglesworth (p. 201), who has been involved in a number of campaign groups advocating for gender equity, most recently PartW.

Willis, Beverly. Beverly Willis Architecture Foundation bwaf.org

American architect Willis has pioneered new technologies in architecture, urban planning and public policy throughout her career. While she is best known for the San Francisco Ballet Building (1984) in California, USA, she is also the founder of the Beverly Willis Architecture Foundation, which works to change the culture for women working in the building industry. The foundation focuses on documenting the work of women in architecture and promoting the leadership of women in professional organizations related to the building industry.

Wilson, Mabel O. Who Builds Your Architecture? whobuilds.org

Wilson is director of transdisciplinary practice Studio &, a co-director of the Global Africa Lab at Columbia University's Graduate School of Architecture and a researcher at the Institute for Research in African-American Studies, also at Columbia. As founder of Who Builds Your Architecture?, Wilson examines the links between labour, architecture and the global networks that form around buildings.

Wright, Gwendolyn. *Building the Dream: A Social History of Housing in America* (Cambridge: MIT Press, 1983)

Wright is professor of architecture at Columbia Graduate School of Architecture, Planning and Preservation in New York, USA, where, in 1985, she was the first woman to receive tenure. Wright has focused principally on American architecture and urbanism from the late nineteenth century to the present day. She has also written extensively about transnational exchanges, especially colonial and more recent neo-colonial aspects of both Modernism and historic preservation.

ENDNOTES

Would They Still Call Me a Diva?

1   Zeuler RM de A. Lima, *Lina Bo Bardi* (New Haven: Yale University Press, 2013). p. 66

2   Watari, Etsuko, ed. *Lina Bo Bardi* (Tokyo: Toto Publishing, 2017). p. 42

3   Despite gaining consent for the scheme the project would not go on site for another three years, with various obstacles delaying its completion until 1969. Bo Bardi, Lina. Quoted in *Stones Against Diamonds*, (London: AA Publications, 2009). p. 121

4   Bardi, Pietro Maria. Quoted in Lima, *Lina Bo Bardi*. p. 71

5   Rand, Ayn. *The Fountainhead* (Indianapolis: Bobbs-Merrill Company, 1943). This image is inscribed in the character of Howard Roark, an architect who represented the ideal man – himself supposedly based on the real-life architect Frank Lloyd Wright.

6   Budds, Diana. 'Architecture Has a Woman Problem', *Fast Company*, 20 December 2017

7   Rawsthorn, Alice. 'The Tortured History of Eileen Gray's Modern Gem', *New York Times*, 25 August 2013

8   Wainwright, Oliver. 'Snubbed, Cheated, Erased: The Scandal of Architecture's Invisible Women', *Guardian*, 16 October 2018

9   Waite, Richard and Mark, Laura. 'BBC Slammed for "Bias" After Patty Hopkins is Sidelined in TV Show', *Architects' Journal*, 5 March 2014

10 Lok Lui, Ann. 'Working in the Shadows', *Archpaper*, 25 April 2012

11 Sherlock, Amy. 'Not Without Struggle', *Frieze Masters*, Issue 7, September 2018.

12 Gridrod, John. 'Jane Drew and Maxwell Fry Talk Chandigarh', *Dirty Modern Scoundrel*, 23 October 2016

13 Grove, Valerie. *The Compleat Women: Marriage, Motherhood, Career, Can She Have It All?* (New York: Vintage Publishing, 1989)

14 MATRIX. *Making Space: Women and the Man Made Environment* (London: Pluto Press, 1987)

15 Taking Place is a group formed of women artists and architects who came together out of a shared interest in questions of gender and spatial practice.

16 Colomina, Beatriz and Bloomer, Jennifer, eds. *Sexuality and Space* (New York: Princeton Architectural Press, 1992)

17 Parlour website: archiparlour.org

18 Matri-Archi(tecture) website: matri-archi.com

19 De Silva, Minnette. *The Life and Work of an Asian Woman Architect* (Colombo: Smart Media Productions, 1998)

Numerals from here refer to page numbers

13 Burrichter, Felix. 'Amale Andraos', *Pin–Up*, Issue 21, Fall Winter 2016/17. p. 96

19 'AR_EA Colombia: Ctrl G Estudio de Arquitectura', *Architectural Review*, 1 October 2015

26 SESC stands for Serviço Social do Comércio (Business Social Service), a Brazilian non-governmental organization created in the 1940s to provide employees with health services, and sporting and cultural activities.

78 Astbury, Jon. 'Clarity of plan and vision: The Cathedral in Sweden by Petra Gipp Arkitektur', *Architectural Review*, 15 March 2016

88 Mairs, Jessica. '"Under-recognised" Itsuko Hasegawa wins inaugural Royal Academy Architecture Prize', *Dezeen*, 8 February 2018

105 Gesualdi, Frank. 'Sharon Johnston and Mark Lee', *Bomb*, 15 July 2017

113 Nimmo, Andrew. 'Something', first published in *Lnxx Lahznimmo Architects a Twenty-Year Retrospective* (2015)

147 Frampton, Kenneth. *Patkau Architects* (Monacelli Press: New York, 2006)

190 Tod Williams Billie Tsien Architects website: 'People', twbta.com

INDEX

PICTURE CREDITS

I would like to thank Assemble for the collective thought and care put into the research for this book, particularly the work of Audrey Thomas-Hayes and Holly Briggs. The majority of the more detailed research was done by Katherine Spence, whose recommendations have been invaluable in attempting to capture the breadth of this topic in one volume. I would also like to acknowledge our indebtedness to those whose work attempts to destabilize the hegemony of gender identifications. The authors who have been particularly influential in shaping our thinking include Audre Lorde, Maggie Nelson, Judith Butler and Donna Haraway.

— Dr Jane Hall

Dr Jane Hall studied architecture at King's College, Cambridge, and the Royal College of Art, London, where she received her PhD in 2018. She was the inaugural recipient of the British Council Lina Bo Bardi Fellowship (2013) and is a founding member of the London-based architecture collective Assemble, who won the Turner Prize (2015) for their work created collaboratively with the residents of Granby Four Streets in Liverpool.

Phaidon Press Limited
Regent's Wharf
All Saints Street
London N1 9PA

Phaidon Press Inc.
65 Bleecker Street
New York, NY 10012

phaidon.com

First Published in 2019
© 2019 Phaidon Press Limited

ISBN 978 0 7148 7927 7

A CIP Catalogue record for this book is available from the British Library and the Library of Congress.

Commissioning Editor: Virginia McLeod
Project Editor: Belle Place
Production Controller: Jane Harman
Cover Design: Pentagram

The Publisher would also like to thank Emma Barton, Robert Davies, Milena Harrison-Gray, Chris Lacy, Ian McDonald and Anthony Naughton for their contributions to the book.

Printed in China